the simple guide to MINI-REEF Aquariums

Jeffrey Kurtz

D0520196

T.F.H. Publications, Inc.
One TFH Plaza
Third and Union Avenues
Neptune City, NJ 07753

Kurtz, Jeffrey.
The simple guide to mini-reefs / Jeffrey Kurtz.
p. cm.
Includes index.
ISBN 0-7938-2121-5 (alk. paper)
1. Marine aquariums. I. Title.
SF457.1.K87 2005
639.34'2--dc22
2004023665

This book has been published with the intent to provide accurate and authoritative information in regard to the subject matter within. While every precaution has been taken in preparation of this book, the author and publisher expressly disclaim responsibility for any errors, omissions, or adverse effects arising from the use or application of the information contained herein. The techniques and suggestions are used at the reader's discretion and are not to be considered a substitute for veterinary care. If you suspect a medical problem, consult your veterinarian.

www.tfhpublications.com

Acknowledgements

I would like to thank my wife, Melissa, for her limitless patience and support during the months I spent writing this book, and my children, Aidan and Hannah, for reducing the noise level of their play to a dull roar whenever I was at work. I would also like to thank my parents, Robert and Mary Ann, for indulging my interest in the aquarium hobby from a very young age and for helping to plant the seed that would eventually burgeon into a lifelong passion.

Special thanks to Dominique DeVito, Brian Scott, Albert Connelly, Jr., and the rest of the staff at T.F.H. Publications, Inc., for giving me the wonderful opportunity to share my thoughts and ideas with my fellow hobbyists. Last, but certainly not least, thanks to all the authors and columnists who have contributed to *Tropical Fish Hobbyist* magazine and the aquarium hobby over the years. Your efforts have been my inspiration.

Contents

Can You
test
for it?

Some inverts are reef-busters

Part One

"Just jump in, Sydney! The water isn't that cold!"

Welcome to the Wonderful World of the Mini-reef!

"A simple guide to mini-reef aquariums"? Sounds like a contradiction in terms, right? After all, a thriving home mini-reef is well beyond the purview of the average aquarist, who lacks a degree in marine biology or chemistry, isn't it?

Well, let me assure you that nothing could be further from the truth. I know this because in my high school days, I failed chemistry, barely passed biology, yet somehow still managed, years later–after getting my feet wet with a few simpler systems first–to succeed with a mini-reef aquarium.

I'm convinced that virtually anyone with a

An aquarium as beautiful as this one is not impossible if you do your research and take your time.

willingness to learn and a basic understanding of sound aquarium practice–achieved through prior experience with freshwater or fish-only marine systems–can build on this knowledge to create their dream mini-reef.

I should point out that lack of prior experience is not necessarily a deal breaker. Some determined individuals with no prior aquarium experience whatsoever can succeed with a mini-reef, given the right attitude and approach. Just be aware that if you fall into this category, you may need to do some serious research to get up to speed on the principles of basic aquarium husbandry before diving in. Hopefully, reading this book will help you get started in the right direction.

The Mini-Reef Defined

Before we immerse ourselves in the minutia of mini-reef maintenance (please excuse the shameless alliteration), let's define for ourselves exactly what a mini-reef aquarium is and how it differs from other saltwater systems.

Mini-reefs are designed to show-case a variety of sessile and motile invertebrates, as well as fishes.

In a nutshell, the mini-reef showcases the many beautiful sessile (attached) invertebrates–primarily corals and their close relatives–that are found on tropical coral reefs, as well as many of the motile (non-attached) ones, too. A bed of live sand is often installed as a substrate–though some aquarists prefer no substrate whatsoever–and live rock is typically used to create the reef framework (don't worry, we'll get into sand beds and live rock in much greater detail later on). With a few exceptions, specialized, high-intensity lighting is required over the mini-reef in order to sustain the light-hungry corals and other invertebrates typically kept in these systems.

Reef-friendly fishes and motile invertebrates (shrimps, crabs, snails, and the like) can be included in the mini-reef, but keep their numbers small in order to minimize their impact on the invertebrate's health and on the system's water quality.

The Fish-only Aquarium

At the other end of the marine aquarium spectrum, you have the fish-only system. As you've undoubtedly deduced already, the fish-only aquarium focuses on the fish of the coral reef rather than on the corals and other invertebrates found there. Various motile invertebrates do occasionally find their way into fish-only systems, which makes the name "fish-only" something of an anomaly. Whether motile invertebrates are included or not, the fish-only system is considerably more forgiving than the mini-reef when it comes to the occasional misstep by the novice marine aquarist. The fish-only aquarium is also considerably less costly than the mini-reef because it's less equipment-intensive, and no special lighting is required to keep the fish happy and healthy.

Live rock and live sand beds are usually not included in the fish-only tank. In years past, fish-only systems were "aquascaped" using bare rock and bleached coral skeletons, giving them a somewhat sterile and artificial appearance. Nowadays, authentic-looking manufactured reef décor makes it possible to create very attractive and naturalistic fish-only systems.

The F.O.W.L.R. Aquarium

The F.O.W.L.R. aquarium, or Fish-Only-With-Live-Rock aquarium, is a sort of compromise between the fish-only tank and the mini-reef. The F.O.W.L.R. aquarium, like the mini-reef, has a foundation of live rock, and possibly live sand, but stops short of including the more challenging coral species. Like the fish-only system, F.O.W.L.R. aquariums may contain motile invertebrates and are typically illuminated with normal-output lamps rather than the high-intensity lighting of the mini-reef.

If you look closely you'll see that the corals in this tank are on the background.

As you might imagine, the F.O.W.L.R. aquarium can be converted rather effortlessly to a mini-reef with the addition of appropriate lighting and livestock and hence makes an excellent jumping off point for the aspiring mini-reef aquarist.

Part 1

As Ye Sow, So Shall Ye Reef!

Live rock and live sand beds? Specialized lighting? Lots of equipment? Sensitive corals? Sounds like the mini-reef is a costly endeavor, doesn't it? Well, there's no getting around the fact that setting up even a basic mini-reef can set you back a few dollars. But in order to succeed, you'll have to make an even greater investment–your time, energy, and attention. In fact, the best, most expensive equipment available makes a sorry substitute for diligent maintenance and careful observation on the part of the budding reef aquarist.

To illustrate this point, I like to draw on the example of a garden. Anyone who has kept a garden knows that you can't just stick a bunch of plants in the ground, water them occasionally, and then expect to enjoy a lush, colorful garden all through the growing season. You've got to mulch, weed, fertilize, turn in compost, prune, deadhead spent blossoms, spray for pests and disease, provide winter protection for delicate plants, and so on if you hope to enjoy ongoing good results. Sure, there are labor-saving products out there that can make gardening easier, but in the end, the amount of elbow grease you put in is the greatest determining factor in your level of gardening success.

The same rule applies to the mini-reef. No amount of automation and high-priced gadgetry can take the place of regular partial water changes, close and frequent observation of livestock, and careful monitoring of water quality. All of these routine maintenance steps are completely within the control of the aquarist, and they pay huge dividends in the form of a beautiful, healthy mini-reef.

Returning to our gardening model, when planning a garden, it's wise to consult with an experienced horticulturist before buying any plant material, so that you're assured of getting compatible species that will thrive in your particular garden setting. For example, if your garden plot has heavy clay soil and no protection from sun and wind, you wouldn't have much success with growing azaleas or other sensitive broadleaf evergreens.

Small-polyped stony corals will need excellent water clarity and quality in order to thrive in your mini-reef.

Well, the same holds true for the mini-reef. Not all coral reef invertebrates come from the same part of the world or from the same zone on a particular reef. So, for example, you wouldn't want to place mushroom polyps, which usually prefer lower light levels, at the top of your mini-reef, just inches away from high-intensity lamps. Nor would you want to place a light- and current-loving *Acropora* coral species in a stagnant area of the tank beneath an overhanging rock. Consulting a qualified aquarium dealer can help you avoid such pitfalls and set you on a course for success with your first mini-reef.

Your Responsibilities as a Reef Keeper

The reef-keeping hobby carries with it significant environmental responsibilities that one would never associate with other pastimes. After all, with the exception of the occasional non-replaced divot, how much impact does the average casual round of golf have on the environment? Responsible reef keepers, on the other hand, must develop a keen awareness of the environmental implications of their hobby–for example, how their livestock is collected, what conditions various corals need to ensure their longevity, how captive propagation can reduce stress on the coral reefs, and so forth.

The choices we make as private reef aquarists when purchasing livestock can impact not only the coral reefs themselves but also our hobby in general. While the collection of reef organisms for the aquarium trade has a minimal impact on the overall health of the reefs when compared to other large-scale influences (e.g., deforestation, overfishing, and recreational diving), it makes a measurable impact nonetheless. So when we as reef aquarists fail to support the captive propagation of corals and reef fish because wild-collected specimens are cheaper, or we continue to purchase animals with poor captive survival records simply because they're too attractive to resist, we give the entire reef-keeping hobby a black eye.

In essence, mini-reef aquarists take organisms adapted to life in one of the earth's most stable, pristine environments and attempt to keep them alive and thriving in a closed, artificial system. It's an awesome undertaking when you think about it, and an awesome responsibility. Those who take this responsibility to heart, do the necessary research, invest a reasonable amount of time and energy, and treat the unique creatures in their care with the utmost consideration are almost assured good results. On the other hand, haphazard maintenance and inattention to aquarium conditions will result in failure. Put another way, the choice to succeed with a mini-reef is really yours to make!

Having said that, I'm going to ask every reader to recite the following solemn "Reef Keeper's Pledge" aloud (you can even raise your right hand if the impulse grabs you) before taking any further steps:

The Reef Keeper's Pledge

I, (your name), being of sound mind and body, do solemnly pledge that I will embark upon the reef-keeping hobby only after thoroughly researching the subject via books, magazines, newsletters, the Internet, fellow reef keepers, and any additional resources available to me.

I understand that a certain cash outlay is unavoidable when embarking upon the mini-reef hobby, and I have informed my spouse/domestic partner of such.

I will proceed with set up slowly and deliberately, enjoying each fascinating step, with the full understanding that only bad things happen quickly in the mini-reef.

I will purchase livestock only after my aquarium has completely cycled—and then, slowly and methodically.

I will never purchase livestock on impulse and then attempt to determine its husbandry requirements later, because I know that this way lies madness.

I understand that corals and other invertebrates need room to grow, and for the well-being of the animals in my care, I will never attempt to keep more than my aquarium can accommodate.

I understand that corals and other reef invertebrates are unique living things that require life-long care. They are not pretty decorations to be replaced with every change in room décor.

I will set aside a reasonable amount of time each day for routine aquarium maintenance chores and water quality testing, scheduling such activities on a calendar if necessary.

I accept the axiom that the water change is the single most valuable tool in the reef keeper's arsenal.

I accept the fact that problems will occasionally arise in my mini-reef, and I will treat each new problem as a challenge to be overcome rather than an insurmountable obstacle.

I will not repeatedly alter my approach to reef keeping with each change in the tide of popular opinion, because that way also lies madness. Besides, if it ain't broke, I shouldn't try to fix it.

I will never abandon the reef-keeping hobby just because the going gets tough. Rather, I will redouble my efforts to master the skills I need to succeed.

In years to come, I will share the wisdom I have acquired with others who wish to enter the mini-reef hobby—and I will do so enthusiastically and without condescension.

I understand that I am embarking upon this wonderful hobby of my own volition and therefore, I accept full responsibility for my ultimate success or failure and for the unique organisms entrusted to my care.

Of course, I'm writing this pledge with tongue in cheek, but only to a certain extent. I'm convinced that anyone approaching the reef-keeping hobby honestly and with eyes wide open has a much greater likelihood of creating a stunningly beautiful slice of coral reef than someone who learns the ins and outs of the hobby through trial and error. Besides, with the trial-and-error approach, many corals and other reef dwellers are likely to be unduly sacrificed along the way, and that is simply not an acceptable price to pay.

C'mon in!
The Water's Fine!

In Chapter One, I repeatedly emphasized the importance of doing copious amounts of research before setting up your mini-reef aquarium. But where should you begin? First, I would strongly urge you to invest in other mini-reef-related books currently available through T.F.H. Publications. For that matter, if you don't already subscribe to *Tropical Fish Hobbyist* magazine, by all means, start your subscription soon! I apologize if I appear biased, but *T.F.H.* has been a veritable treasure trove of aquarium information for me over the years, and I continue to learn something new with each issue.

Internet Research

Internet reef-keepers' forums are also great

Research, research, and more research will be needed to get your mini-reef into tiptop condition.

sources of information for the aspiring mini-reef aquarist—especially when you need faster answers than are possible with periodical print media. For example, let's assume your local aquarium dealer is offering a great deal on a particular lighting system and you'd like to find out whether others in the hobby have had success with that system. Posting your question on a reef-keeping forum will usually bring a variety of responses in very short order, which is a benefit that our reef-keeping forebears—the pioneers of our hobby—could only dream of.

But let me add this one caveat when it comes to online forums: Opinions about reef-keeping techniques are as numerous as the stars, and it's not uncommon to receive starkly conflicting advice within a single thread. Often, a seemingly innocuous question (such as, What's the best method for supplementing calcium to your aquarium?) can lead to a prolonged heated dispute—or "flame war"—between two or more parties in the forum. When such disputes arise, and all sides of the argument seem perfectly plausible, it can be very difficult for a novice reef keeper to determine the best course of action to follow.

A Trusted Aquarium Dealer

In these days of Internet shopping, it's possible to purchase virtually everything you need to set up and stock a mini-reef aquarium from online vendors. The only problem is, while you may get better prices online, you can't often get one-on-one help when you really need it. After all, it's pretty hard to get face time from a faceless vendor.

A trusted local dealer, on the other hand, can be very informative and reassuring as you begin working with unfamiliar products and equipment, and he's just a quick phone call or car ride away. Sure, you might have to pay a bit more when you buy aquarium goods from a small retailer, but the added cost is well worth it when you factor in the valuable hobbyist-dealer relationship. I should also mention that your local dealer will, in all likelihood, be the first person you turn to when you're ready to sell or trade the coral fragments (or "frags") that you'll eventually harvest from your thriving mini-reef!

Don't Forget Your Fellow Reefers!

Last but not least, you can always seek out fellow reef aquarium enthusiasts (reefers) for additional advice on getting your mini-reef started and stocked. Consider joining a local aquarium club or society that meets in your area. Can't locate any? Consider starting a club of your own. Most experienced reef keepers are more than willing to play the role of mentor so they can bestow the wisdom they've acquired upon those who are new to the hobby. Most beginners appreciate the opportunity to meet other novice aquarists who share the same skill level and newfound enthusiasm.

Along with imparting the wisdom of their experience, many reef keepers are happy to share the fruits of their reef-keeping labor (i.e., extra coral frags) with others in the hobby. Many a budding reef aquarist has stocked his first mini-reef–at very low cost, if not for free, I might add–with coral frags acquired from fellow reefers. Of course, once you've experienced some success in growing and propagating your own corals, you might be expected to return the favor, but that's the beauty of the coral barter system–everybody benefits, even the corals!

Exploring Options for Mini-Reef Magnitude

Now that we've touched on the various resources available to the aspiring reef aquarist, let's dive right in and begin exploring the various size options you can choose from for your new mini-reef.

Aquarium Size

In most aquarium literature that I've read, newcomers to the mini-reef hobby are encouraged to start out with the biggest aquarium they can reasonably afford and accommodate in their living quarters. The reasoning behind this is that a larger volume of water affords the aquarist much greater stability in water parameters–and, hence, a significantly greater margin of error–than does a smaller volume of water. In other words, changes in water temperature, pH, alkalinity, dissolved pollutant levels, and other important parameters will occur at a much slower rate in a large body of water than they will in a small one. So, by logical extension, common beginner errors, such as overfeeding the aquarium inhabitants or accidentally overdosing an additive (did that say add one teaspoon per 75

Make sure to choose an aquarium that will be of proper size for what you plan to keep in it.

gallons of tank capacity or one tablespoon?) will have less of an impact on water quality in a larger volume of water.

I largely encourage the bigger-is-better approach when setting up your first mini-reef aquarium. So what constitutes bigger? I'd recommend starting out with a 55-gallon tank at the very least; 75 or 100 gallons of tank capacity would be even better. Not only will a larger tank provide greater stability in water conditions, but it will also allow you to keep more corals and other reef invertebrates without too much crowding. And what reef keeper in his or her right mind could argue with that?

A Note About Nano-Reefs

Having said all that, setting up a large aquarium is just not in the cards for many people due to limited space, rental agreements, money, or other prohibitions. So does that mean the space-impaired must forgo keeping a mini-reef altogether? Nope, not at all. In fact, one of the fastest-growing trends in the reef-keeping hobby today is the so-called nano-reef, which is commonly defined as any reef aquarium smaller than 20 gallons. Reef aquarists who are looking to really downsize can go with a pico-reef, which is any reef aquarium under five gallons. Many aquarists have even succeeded with pico-reefs in less than a gallon of water!

Small Frags, like this Zoanthid polyp, make excellent additions to a nano-reef tank.

Advantages of the nano-reef include very low initial setup cost (around $200 or less, on average), portability (it's the perfect office or dorm room aquarium), and ease of maintenance. Also, most commonly kept soft corals, stony corals, and reef-friendly fish can be maintained successfully in a nano-reef.

But nanos have their negatives, too. As I've mentioned, water conditions deteriorate much more rapidly in a smaller volume of water, so the smaller the nano, the more difficult it is to maintain excellent water quality–and therefore, the more frequently you must perform partial water changes. In addition, nanos are, not surprisingly, very limiting in the number of specimens you can maintain, especially when it comes to fish. In fact, many experienced nano-reef keepers wisely discourage the inclusion of fish in any tank under 5 gallons.

If you're like me and you enjoy observing a diverse mini-reef ecosystem, then you might not be satisfied with a nano-reef tank. On the other hand, if you prefer to focus your energy and attention on a few select species, you might be perfectly content going nano.

The Shape of Things to Come

While the capacity of a tank is an important consideration when setting up a mini-reef, the actual shape of the tank plays a major role as well. For example, a long, low, rectangular tank is preferable to a tall hexagonal tank of the same capacity. Why is this so? First, the rectangular tank has a larger surface area that is exposed to ambient air, which allows for more efficient gas exchange and, hence, more efficient oxygenation and venting of noxious gasses.

Second, the rectangular tank, being significantly shallower than the hex tank, allows more light of the correct spectrum to reach corals and other light-hungry invertebrates at all levels of the tank. In a taller aquarium, on the other hand, the corals placed in the lower regions might not receive adequate illumination, depending on their needs.

Aquariums come in a variety of shapes and sizes.

I should point out that this isn't necessarily a problem for the reef keeper who chooses to mix both soft corals and stony corals in the same tank. Soft corals, which don't typically demand the same intense level of illumination as stony corals, can be positioned in the lower half of the tank, while the stony corals can be placed at the top half, directly under the lights. However, for the aquarist who wants to keep mostly stony corals and perhaps a *Tridacna* clam or two, this arrangement would be less than optimal, because nothing would thrive in the lower half of the tank.

A third consideration is that it's a heck of a lot easier to reach the bottom of a low, rectangular tank for routine maintenance purposes (e.g., to scrape algae from the glass or to retrieve a dropped aquarium brush) than it is with a tall, hexagonal tank.

But if you're bent on setting up a taller tank, there's no reason you can't, as long as you take these design limitations (as described above) into consideration when stocking. Also, the drawback of reduced gas exchange can be overcome somewhat by installing a rectangular sump beneath the main display aquarium.

Glass or Acrylic?

When shopping for your mini-reef tank, you'll have the option of glass or acrylic construction. Which is the better choice? Well, there's no right or wrong answer to that question. Both glass and acrylic tanks have their advantages and disadvantages, and the best choice for you depends on your particular set of circumstances.

Generally speaking, glass tanks are less expensive than acrylic tanks of the same size, but they're also much heavier and more prone to cracking, shattering, or springing leaks. That being said, with proper handling (and leveling prior to filling), modern glass aquariums seldom break or spring leaks, even after many years of use. And besides, you just can't beat the cost of glass!

Acrylic tanks offer superior image clarity and structural durability. They're also significantly lighter and provide better thermal insulation than glass tanks. Acrylic is also relatively easy to drill, in case you want to install a standpipe or overflow. The only real downside to acrylic, apart from its higher price tag, is that it can be scratched quite easily when you're scraping stubborn coralline algae or performing other routine maintenance chores.

Selecting a Stand

I won't bore you with a prolonged dissertation on the ins and outs of purchasing an aquarium stand for your mini-reef. As long as the stand is rated to support the weight of your aquarium and is not constructed of metal, which will rust in short order when exposed to salt creep (an inevitable byproduct of any mini-reef), you can't really go wrong. Those critical considerations aside, the choice of stand is essentially a stylistic one.

I went with an inexpensive cabinet-style stand constructed of yellow pine to support my 75-gallon display tank. It's nothing spectacular to look at, but at the same time, I don't worry too much about occasionally spilling saltwater on it. Besides, in spite of its modest appearance, it's held up quite nicely for many years now, and besides, I'm more concerned with the appearance of the inside of my tank than the outside, anyway.

Site Considerations

Before putting your tank, stand, or any other equipment in place, it's critical to survey your selected location carefully to ensure that it's suitable for supporting a fully functioning aquarium for the long haul. Ask yourself the following questions:

• Can the floor support the weight of the aquarium once it has been filled with water (consider that each gallon of saltwater adds approximately 8.5 pounds)?

• Can the adjacent floor covering, woodwork, wall treatments, furnishings, etc. endure the inevitable salt spray and the occasional saltwater spill?

• Are there sufficient electrical outlets in close proximity, and are they protected with Ground Fault Circuit Interrupters (GFCIs)?

• Are the outlets connected to a circuit that can accommodate all the necessary filtration and lighting equipment without causing an overload?

Always be sure to check the level of the tank BEFORE you add water to it!

• Will you have the freedom to add more electrical devices in the future, if necessary?

• Is the location free of registers, vents, and other heating or cooling sources that might adversely affect water temperature stability?

• Is the location within reasonable proximity to a water source and drain?

• Is the overhead clearance sufficient to allow proper ventilation and to accommodate a lighting fixture?

Your local aquarium dealer can assist you in choosing the proper equipment for your application.

• Are shelves or cabinets handy so you can store test kits, cleaning implements, additives, and other accessories?

If you've answered each of these questions in the affirmative, then you can rest assured that you've selected a good location for your mini-reef.

Now it's time to move on to the setup phase. Go ahead and set the tank on its stand, and do any final measuring that is necessary to ensure proper distance from walls, doorways, and so on. Be sure to leave adequate space behind the tank so you can fit tubing, electrical cords, perhaps a hang-on-tank refugium or overflow for your sump, and any additional equipment you might choose to add later on. Remember, it's better to have the space and not need it than to need the space and not have it.

Once you're completely satisfied with the position of your tank, check to make sure it's on-the-bubble level. At this point, many aquarists choose to add a thin layer of cushioning material between the tank and the stand to aid in leveling. If the tank is not level and you proceed to fill it with substrate, live rock, and water, your beautiful new mini-reef may eventually spring a leak due to the uneven pressure exerted on the seams by the water.

The Cost Question

Having purchased your tank and stand and most likely having done a little shopping around for the other equipment and accessories that you're ultimately going to need, you've undoubtedly come to the conclusion–as I did when embarking upon this hobby– that setting up a mini-reef is no cheap undertaking. Well, let me offer a little reassurance on this matter. There's no question that a mini-reef can be expensive to set up and maintain, but by making wise purchases at the outset and avoiding unnecessary bells and whistles, just about anyone can afford a modest mini-reef. Wherever possible throughout this book, I'll offer cost-cutting hints to help ease your sticker shock.

Live Sand Beds

For most reef keepers, the allure of a mini-reef is having a little slice of ocean to observe and enjoy at home (and show off to their friends) any time they want. Often what draws people to this hobby is having experienced a natural coral reef firsthand, perhaps while snorkeling or scuba diving in some exotic tropical locale, or having seen stunning coral reef images on television or in books and magazines. The tendency when setting up a mini-reef system is to attempt to replicate the look and, to the extent possible, the function of a natural coral reef. So it seems logical that a mini-reef aquarium should have some sort of sand-based substrate just like one would find surrounding coral reefs in the wild, right?

Sand beds in the mini-reef afford the hobbyist a solid foundation in which to build a reef on.

The Great Substrate Debate!

Well, this brings us to the first controversy of reef keeping: the Great Substrate Debate! As with many facets of the mini-reef hobby, there are wildly disparate views about how much substrate, if any, should be used. And, as you'll notice with many of the topics we'll discuss in this book, the approach that is considered dogmatic one year often becomes heresy a year or so later.

Some Say No Way!

When I first became interested in marine aquariums, the accepted practice, when it came to substrates in mini-reefs, was to avoid them altogether. While this left the bottom glass pane of the aquarium exposed, an attractive growth of coralline algae would eventually cover it, or the aquarist might choose to install just a sprinkling of sand to conceal the bottom glass.

And there was solid logic behind this approach: While coral reefs teem with a staggering diversity of life, the waters surrounding them are surprisingly devoid of dissolved nutrients. Any nutrients that are produced–for example, the byproducts of waste from fish, corals, and other reef organisms–are instantly diluted by the essentially limitless volume of water and then transported away by ocean currents.

Aquariums can be maintained with or without a sand bed. In the end, it's your choice.

However, in the closed system of the mini-reef, dissolved nutrients and other pollutants tend to accumulate, to the detriment of the corals and other reef organisms–until the next water change, anyway. Dissolved nutrients also fuel outbreaks of undesirable algae–especially the dreaded hair algae–which drive many reef keepers to distraction and, in extreme cases, out of the hobby.

So proponents of the substrate-free approach believe that, since sand and other substrate materials tend to trap uneaten food, fish feces, and other forms of detritus, which then decompose and release nutrients into the water, it is best to dispense with sand beds altogether. With no substrate to trap it, organic debris remains suspended in the water column, where it can be removed from the aquarium via the filtration system. It logically follows, then, that such systems rely heavily on water movement, mechanical filtration, and frequent siphoning by the aquarist to export organic debris.

Many a mini-reef was established using the substrate-free approach, and many a mini-reefer still practices this method with success today. However, other schools of thought have arisen that favor the use of sand beds–and deep ones, at that.

Some Lay it on Thick!

Deep sand beds (or DSBs) came into vogue with the advent of more natural reef-keeping methods, such as the Berlin method and Jaubert's natural nitrate reduction technique (more detail on both later), which depend less on high-tech water purification gadgets and more on the biological processes occurring within the aquarium.

A DSB is typically three to four inches deep–though there is much disagreement about the optimum depth (some say it should be as deep as six inches)–and is composed of sugar-fine coral or aragonite sand.

To aid in your calculations when purchasing sand, consider that using ten pounds of sand per square foot of bottom area will yield an approximate depth of one inch. So, for the sake of illustration, a tank with a bottom dimension of 48 inches by 18 inches (actually, the inside dimensions would probably be 47.5 inches by 17.5 inches, but you get the idea) would have a total area

Many hobbyists use macroalgae in place of deep sand beds (DSBs).

Live sand may be purchased at your local aquarium supplier.

of six square feet. Thus, you would need to purchase 180 pounds of sand to create a three-inch-deep sand bed.

It's highly desirable to have a thriving population of tiny organisms–worms, mollusks, crustaceans, and echinoderms–as well as beneficial microorganisms in a healthy DSB. This complement of microscopic critters and sand-stirring beasties is introduced into the DSB by incorporating "live sand."

Live Sand

What exactly is live sand? Essentially, it is coral sand–complete with the aforementioned desirable organisms–that is harvested near coral reefs. It is not simply sand taken out of the ocean. Just because sand is collected from the ocean floor does not mean it is desirable, or even safe, for use in your mini-reef.

For instance, sand harvested too close to shore is likely to be contaminated with pollutants from boat traffic, fertilizer or pesticide runoff from agriculture, sewage discharged from the mainland, and disease-causing microorganisms. One of the most common pathogens is the *Vibrio* virus, which is known to cause rapid tissue necrosis (RTN) in many small-polyped stony corals.

Live sand is filled with various organisms that assist in breaking down harmful wastes.

As with anything worthwhile, quality live sand isn't cheap, so creating a DSB using only live sand can be cost prohibitive, especially with larger aquarium systems. To get around this, most experienced reefers use mostly non-live sand and "seed" it with a smaller quantity of live sand (up to a ratio of 50/50). Over time, the beneficial beasties proliferate and spread throughout the entire sand bed. Incidentally, a DSB that consists entirely of live sand or has become live is often referred to in reef-keeping parlance as a DLSB, or deep live sand bed–yet another of the many perplexing acronyms you'll encounter in the reef-keeping hobby!

One caveat about non-live sand: Make sure the sand you use does not contain silicates, which promote the growth of troublesome algae. This rules out the use of the inexpensive play sand sold at most home-and-garden retail stores. Stick with coral or aragonite sand instead. It's more costly at the outset, but it will save you untold hours of doing battle with plague algae later on. Besides, the white color of coral or aragonite sand imparts a much more naturalistic look than play sand does.

Installing Live Sand

When adding bags of live sand to your mini-reef, you'll want to start with the tank at least half filled with saltwater. After opening the top of the first bag, cautiously lower it to the bottom of the tank, clasping your hand over the opening to contain the sand. Then, gently tip the bag over on its side and carefully begin pouring the contents on top of the non-live sand below (assuming you're "seeding" a non-live bed with live sand). Using your hands, gingerly spread the live sand evenly over the bottom layer. Remember, you're using sugar-fine sand, so some clouding is inevitable. However, if you just dump the sand in carelessly, your water will quickly turn milky white. This amount of clouding isn't harmful, but it will prevent you from moving on to the next phase of setup until the fine particles have had a chance to settle out of suspension.

What Does a DSB Do?

So, we've examined the characteristics of a healthy deep sand bed and the preferred method for installing live sand, but apart from creating a natural-looking substrate, what exactly is the purpose of a DSB? For one thing, the tiny organisms in the sand help to consume any uneaten food or other organic matter that settles into the sand before it has a chance to decompose and foul the water. The tiny critters also provide a supplemental live food source for the fish and any invertebrates that are adapted to feed on zooplankton. However, the most significant role a DSB plays is denitrification.

What exactly is denitrification and what does it have to do with your mini-reef? Well, before we delve into that topic, it would behoove us to broach the topic of nitrification–otherwise we're putting the cart before the horse, so to speak.

Know Your Nitrogen Cycle!

The most important biological process that occurs in an aquarium–mini-reef or otherwise–is the nitrogen cycle, which is the basis for the biological filtration methods that we will discuss later in this book. If you can't remember learning about the nitrogen cycle in your high school biology class (I certainly can't, but then it might have come up during one of my naps), it goes something like this:

The cycle begins when ammonia (NH_4) is introduced to the water via animal waste, uneaten food or other organic material that has begun to decompose, or the natural metabolic processes of aquatic organisms. Pure ammonia is highly toxic to aquatic marine organisms and especially deleterious to corals and other reef invertebrates, which demand near-pristine water conditions in order to thrive.

Fortunately, when conditions are right for their proliferation, colonies of beneficial, aerobic nitrifying bacteria quickly convert ammonia to a slightly less harmful compound called nitrite (NO_2), which is slightly less toxic than ammonia but still dangerous to marine organisms. Once nitrite is produced, another group of nitrifying bacteria goes to work and converts the nitrite to nitrate. Nitrate (NO_3) is even less toxic than nitrite. However, while marine fish seem unaffected by nitrate at moderate levels, corals and other sessile invertebrates cannot tolerate it. Nitrate also fuels the growth of unwanted algae. Therefore, in a mini-reef, nitrate must be diluted through water changes until it is undetectable through testing, or it must be removed from the system via denitrification–which brings us back to our deep sand bed.

Up until now, the beneficial nitrifying bacteria we've been discussing have been aerobic, which means they require oxygen in order to proliferate. Hence, they are abundant on any aquarium surface that is exposed to oxygenated water–the glass, rockwork, substrate surface, etc. But in order to complete the nitrogen cycle, we have to call upon denitrifying bacteria, which thrive in anoxic (very low oxygen) conditions.

An oxygen gradient exists within a DSB (i.e., the oxygen concentration is relatively high at the surface but gradually decreases with increasing sand depth). Deep within the sand bed, anoxic conditions prevail, allowing the colonization of denitrifying bacteria. This third complement of beneficial bacteria converts nitrate to free nitrogen and oxygen gasses, which are then released to the atmosphere at the surface of the aquarium, thereby completing the nitrogen cycle.

Mistaken DSB Methodology

DSBs do a wonderful job of nitrate reduction; however, they do have their drawbacks.

Actually, I should modify that statement somewhat. A better way to phrase it might be, DSBs have their drawbacks when incorrect sand bed methodology is employed.

For example, if you use low-quality live sand, the DSB won't contain a healthy complement of burrowing and tunneling creatures, which continually turn over the top layer of sand. Without this sand-stirring activity, the sand will tend to clump together so that nitrate-laden water cannot reach the anoxic zone, where denitrification occurs. Also, without an adequate population of live sand organisms, detritus that settles into the DSB will not be broken down efficiently and completely.

Aragonite is sometimes incorporated into the DSB methodology.

Poor sand bed methodology can also lead to a DSB that operates as a "nutrient sink"; in other words, a sand bed that traps excessive amounts of detritus, which then decomposes and releases excessive nitrate into the water. But this potential problem can be avoided by providing ample water movement within the aquarium. Water movement–through strategically positioned powerheads–keeps organic waste in suspension, where it can be removed via the filtration system or siphoning on the part of the aquarist. The aforementioned healthy population of sand-stirring critters and microorganisms will also help to prevent the "nutrient sink syndrome" by breaking down the detritus before it has a chance to decompose.

Insufficient sand depth is yet another common mistake in DSB methodology that impairs its function. When the depth of a sand bed is maintained below the minimum three inches, it is both too deep to be completely aerobic and too shallow for denitrifying bacteria to set up shop. As a result, the aquarist has to contend with many of the DSB's drawbacks without enjoying any of its benefits.

Plenum Systems

A variation on the DSB that enjoyed widespread popularity among reef keepers for several years is the plenum system. Based on the natural nitrate reduction (NNR) method

Corals, anemones, and macroalgae may all share an aquarium equally if the setup is stable.

conceived in the 1980s by Dr. Jean Jaubert of the University of Nice, plenums were all the rage up until just a few years ago, when aquarists began second-guessing their value or eschewing them altogether.

Like DSBs, plenum systems have their drawbacks—for example, the aforementioned nutrient sink syndrome, or even the production of deadly hydrogen sulfide gas—when installed or maintained incorrectly. On the other hand, like so many controversial reef-keeping practices, many reefers still swear by this technique and have succeeded with it for many years.

A plenum system is essentially a DSB with one significant difference: Before the sand bed is installed, a grid, or plenum, made out of an aquarium-friendly material such as eggcrate (an inexpensive plastic grate used for light diffusion) or a plastic undergravel filter plate, is positioned at the bottom of the tank. The grid is elevated approximately one inch off the bottom using sections of PVC tubing or other suitable materials, which are attached with cable ties or aquarium-safe silicone adhesive. The plenum is then wrapped with screening material, preferably fiberglass window screening. Finally, a three-inch sand bed is installed and seeded with live sand. Depending on the aquarist's preference, a second layer of screening material may be installed on top of the first two inches of sand before adding the final one-inch layer. The purpose of the screen around the grid material is to prevent sand from filling up the plenum, thereby reducing its efficiency. The second screen that divides the substrate prevents burrowing and tunneling organisms found in the top layer—not to mention any burrowing fish that are kept in the mini-reef, such as various wrasses or jawfishes—from disturbing the denitrifying bacteria that are colonizing the lower substrate.

The Purpose of a Plenum

In very simple terms, the plenum creates a stagnant, anoxic layer of water at the bottom of the tank, which encourages the proliferation of denitrifying bacteria in the lowest layer of substrate just above the plenum. Nitrate-laden water diffuses slowly through the sand until it reaches the deepest layer, where the nitrate is converted to free nitrogen gas. The nitrogen gas then rises up through the sand bed and escapes to the surface of the aquarium, where it is released harmlessly into the atmosphere.

Right now you might be asking yourself, why go to all that trouble assembling a complicated plenum system when a DSB will accomplish the same thing with less initial effort? Well, to some extent, that is precisely why plenums have recently been abandoned in favor of the DSB method. Many reef aquarists who have experimented with both approaches see no substantial advantage to a plenum over a DSB. However, those aquarists who have experienced outstanding nitrate reduction results from plenum systems are, understandably, still proponents of their use.

Which type of substrate do I prefer for the mini-reef: no substrate, DSB, or plenum? Well, since I only have experience with the substrate-free and DSB methods, and since my current 75-gallon mini-reef has a thriving three-inch DSB (which, thus far, has done a relatively good job of nitrate reduction), I'd have to throw my support behind the DSB by default. But as with so many aspects of reef keeping, it's important to remember that each approach to the mini-reef substrate has its advantages and disadvantages, and there's no one method that's right for every aquarist under all circumstances.

Live Rock—Building on a Solid Foundation

Now that we've explored the various substrate options for the mini-reef, we can begin to discuss the building material you'll need to use in order to create a natural-looking reef structure that both supports your corals and other sessile invertebrates and provides suitable habitat and shelter for your fish. The "building material" I'm referring to here is called live rock.

What Makes Live Rock Live?

Live rock? Isn't that another contradiction in terms? Well, not exactly. Just like live sand, it's not the rocks themselves that are alive but, rather, the organisms that encrust the surfaces of the rocks and inhabit every tiny pore, crevice, and crease.

Live rock is the most common base on which to set corals in a mini-reef aquarium.

Part 1

Live rocks are extremely porous chunks of coral rubble that break away from the reef–usually as a result of powerful storm surge–and then settle to the sand around the reef, where they become inhabited by a myriad of miniscule marine organisms. Various worms, snails, sponges, tunicates, bryozoans, sea stars, brittle stars, amphipods, microalgae, macroalgae, nitrifying bacteria, and denitrifying bacteria are just a sampling of the fauna and flora known to live on or within live rocks.

Live Rock Sticker Shock

When you begin shopping around for live rock, two facts will occur to you almost immediately: One, there is an incredible diversity of products out there sold under the name "live rock," and two, the stuff can be remarkably expensive.

In fact, when I offhandedly mentioned to a non-aquarist friend how much I'd spent on 90 pounds of live rock for my 75-gallon mini-reef, his jaw just about hit the floor. "You spent that much on a bunch of rocks?" he asked incredulously. "Man, what did your wife say?" Well, I won't repeat what she said, but in my defense, I did manage to save a substantial amount by purchasing it in bulk rather than piecemeal.

Caveat Emptor

While there's no getting around the fact that quality live rock is expensive, there's no reason you have to get soaked when you buy it, either. Look at all your options, and don't be afraid to ask your fellow reefers for their input. An online reef-keepers' forum is the perfect place to start, and you will find a wealth of information there, so that when you go to order your rock at the local fish shop, you will be well informed.

Above all, when you're ready to make this critical investment, keep in mind that old Latin admonition, caveat emptor–let the buyer beware. Too often, less-than-conscientious dealers offer low-quality base rock for sale as "live rock." Base rock is unattractive, non-live rock that is often placed beneath the more valuable live rock specimens in the reef structure as a cost-

Premium live rock is usually encrusted with coralline algae, which may make it more expensive.

cutting measure. But while it certainly can serve a purpose in the mini-reef, base rock cannot be used interchangeably with quality live rock and certainly does not warrant the same level of expenditure. The more educated you are about purchasing live rock, the better off you will be when it's time to go shopping.

The Traits of Quality Live Rock

As you can probably imagine, the quality–and by logical extension, the cost–of live rock varies according to the diversity of life found upon it, the method used in handling and shipping the rock, and the shape and character of the rock itself.

Live rock that exhibits ample evidence of life–feather duster worms, a nice patina of pink and purple coralline algae, various *Caulerpa* or *Halimeda* macroalgae, zoanthid polyps, etc.–is much preferred to rock that is essentially devoid of visible life. In fact, live rock is often classified according to the predominant species growing upon it. For instance, "plant rock" is typically encrusted with various forms of macroalgae, while "zoanthid rock" is encrusted with–you guessed it–zoanthid polyps.

However, abundant growth on live rock isn't always a desirable thing. For example, rock that is coated with a lush growth of filamentous green hair algae (something I've witnessed on more than one occasion) is to be avoided at all cost. Hair algae will quickly proliferate to epidemic proportions under the high-intensity lighting of a mini-reef aquarium, and this irksome, coral-smothering plague can be very challenging to eradicate once it gains a foothold in your tank.

Live base rock may not look as pretty as premium live rock, but it will serve much the same purpose.

Live rock that is kept constantly immersed in water from the point of collection until it arrives on the sales floor is of higher quality than rock shipped "dry" (i.e., wrapped in moist newspaper). I should point out that dry-shipping live rock is a perfectly acceptable practice, but it does necessitate additional "curing" time–even with so-called pre-cured rock–due to the ongoing die-off that occurs in transit. With rock that is kept immersed, on the other hand, more of the desirable encrusting organisms are likely to survive shipping and become established in your mini-reef.

Even the shape of live rock figures into its quality and price. Lightweight, branching, porous rock is prized above heavy, dense, slab-like rock. The former is conducive to attractive and natural-looking aquascaping and provides a significantly greater overall surface area than does the latter. And remember, the greater the surface area, the greater the potential for colonization by beneficial nitrifying and denitrifying bacteria.

Where in the World Does Live Rock Come From?

Live rock is brought to the United States from several Indo-Pacific regions, such as Fiji, Samoa, and the Marshall Islands, as well as from areas closer to home, such as the Caribbean and Gulf of Mexico. In the past, live rock was also collected from the waters around Florida, but nowadays, wild collection of live rock is prohibited there. Fortunately, it's perfectly legal to aquaculture live rock in Florida waters, and many enterprising individuals are now doing just that, so reef aquarists in the U.S. can once again purchase quality live rock that doesn't have to be shipped all the way from overseas.

Look closely and you will see many types of living organisms on premium live rock.

Wild-collected vs. Aquacultured Live Rock

Speaking of aquaculture, this is the perfect time to make my pitch for environmentally-friendly reef keeping. Your first opportunity to make a sound environmental purchase for your mini-reef is when choosing a source for live rock. As with the wild collection of marine fish, corals, and other reef organisms, live rock can be harvested either scrupulously or unscrupulously, using either sustainable or unsustainable methods. If you choose to stock your mini-reef with wild-collected rock, it's highly recommended that you find out as much as you can about the how that rock was collected before buying. Some overseas collectors gather only rock that was broken from the reefs through the forces of nature, while others actively break rock from the living reef itself. This latter method, if not carefully regulated, can do irreparable damage to large tracts of natural reef.

As an environmentally-friendly (or friendlier, anyway) alternative, you can opt to stock your mini-reef with aquacultured live rock, so you'll know with certainty that no harm was done to the coral reefs, which, as we all know, already face considerable stresses and challenges.

The process of aquaculturing live rock is relatively simple–if you leave out most of the mind-numbing bureaucratic details, that is. Essentially the live rock operator scouts out a suitable site on the ocean floor that complies with strict governmental criteria. He then builds an artificial reef by stacking porous, irregularly shaped rocks (usually limestone) atop some form of biodegradable underlayment. The underlayment (e.g., untreated wood lattice or concrete slabs) keeps the lowest rocks in the pile from settling into the sand. Within three to five years, the rock is encrusted with the desired organisms and is ready for harvest and shipping–unless, of course, a hurricane or tropical storm unceremoniously blows the pile to kingdom come, which is not an uncommon occurrence.

One drawback to aquacultured live rock is that, since the limestone rock used in the aquaculture process is typically mined terrestrially, it often has a more rounded or slab-like shape than the wonderfully gnarled, wild-collected rock that hails from, say, Samoa or Fiji. However, this is a small tradeoff when you consider that aquacultured rock has a much smaller impact on the natural reef environment.

Also, many enterprising, land-locked reef aquarists are learning to culture their own live rock in large vats or other containers, using either terrestrially mined rock or "homemade" rocks that are manufactured using various concrete recipes.

Pre-cured vs. Uncured Live Rock

You'll notice when shopping for live rock that you have a choice between "pre-cured" and "uncured" rock–and that the uncured stuff usually costs a heck of a lot less. So what's the difference, and which type is best for your mini-reef?

Well, let's look at it this way: Live rock must always be cured before it is placed in the mini-reef, so, essentially, you can go with both types and get the same results, provided you don't skip this critical step.

As we've discussed, quality live rock collected fresh from the ocean, whether wild-collected or aquacultured, has an incredible diversity of life encrusting it. However, not all

The curing process may take several weeks depending on how "clean" of decaying organisms the rock is.

of these encrusting organisms will survive from the point of collection until the rock has been acclimated to the aquarium. That means a certain amount of die-off is inevitable on all live rock.

Curing is simply the process of allowing this die-off to occur under controlled conditions before it is introduced to the mini-reef. With pre-cured rock, the live rock operator handles this process before selling his product to consumers. With uncured rock, the consumer must do the curing. It's important to understand, though, that even pre-cured rock will go through additional die-off–albeit considerably less than with uncured rock–by the time it reaches the consumer. Hence, some curing on the part of the consumer is unavoidable.

Fortunately, this additional die-off that occurs with pre-cured rock can be used to the aquarist's advantage during the all-important "cycling" phase that must take place before any invertebrates can be introduced to the mini-reef. We'll examine this benefit in much greater detail in the chapter about cycling.

Curing Live Rock
You'll need to have a few tools and other items on hand for the process of curing your live rock. These include:

• Plastic tarp

• Stiff-bristled scrub brush

• Stiff-bristled toothbrush

• Plastic spray bottle

• Large plastic bin

• Small plastic bucket or similar container

• Powerhead or recirculating pump suitable for use in saltwater

• Ammonia, nitrite, and nitrate test kits

When you pick up your live rock, unpack it immediately, and spread the rocks out on the plastic tarp. If you can do this outdoors, so much the better, but it can be performed indoors with the proper precautions.

Fill the plastic bucket about 3/4 full and the large plastic bin approximately halfway with saltwater. Make sure the bin is in a position where you want the curing to occur before filling. (Keep in mind that the curing process can be a smelly affair and that a large plastic bin filled with water and rocks is extremely difficult to move.) Then fill the plastic spray bottle with saltwater.

With the rocks spread out on the tarp and the plastic spray bottle in hand, scan the entire assortment for any undesirable critters that might emerge from the rock–mantis shrimp, bristleworms, stone crabs, etc.–and remove them with considerable caution (i.e., not with your bare hands). Be aware that some of these organisms can inflict a painful sting or wound. If you are unsure whether an animal you see is safe for the mini-reef or not, err on the side of caution and remove it. As you perform this function, mist the rocks frequently with saltwater from the plastic spray bottle to keep them from drying out, especially if you're working outdoors in sunlight.

Cured rock is often less colorful than uncured rock, but with proper care, the rock will soon be beautiful.

Next, with scrub brush, toothbrush, and saltwater-filled bucket handy, examine each rock for dead or dying organisms and brush these off completely, dipping the rock in saltwater to rinse. The larger scrub brush can be used for cleaning off decay on exposed surfaces, while the toothbrush is ideal for reaching into crevices that the scrub brush can't. Sponges, whether dead or alive, should be removed, as they usually will not survive exposure to air and hence, will eventually die and decompose anyway.

Once you're satisfied that you've removed as much of the dead or dying matter as possible, you can place the rock into the large plastic bin, which has now become your "curing vat." If necessary, add more saltwater to the bin to ensure that the cleaned rocks are completely submerged. Place the powerhead or re-circulating pump into the bin and position it so that water continually circulates throughout the rocks.

While curing, perform frequent water changes to remove harmful byproducts. After all, you paid a hefty sum for all those encrusting organisms, and you don't want to lose them to dissolved pollutants.

To monitor the curing process, you'll need to put your ammonia, nitrite, and nitrate test kits to good use. First, test for the presence of ammonia, which will spike in short order due to the continued die-off that you weren't able to get off (there is always some). After the ammonia spike, consecutive tests over several days should reveal a gradual drop in the ammonia level, which means that nitrifying bacteria have begun to convert the ammonia to nitrite. You should then observe a spike in nitrite and a gradual drop in the ammonia level. Finally, nitrate will spike as the nitrite level drops to zero. When ammonia and nitrite are no longer detectable and a careful "sniff test" indicates that no further die-off is occurring, the rock is considered cured.

How long does the curing process take? That depends on several factors, including how thoroughly you scrubbed away decaying organisms beforehand and how much organic debris you removed during partial water changes, but you can expect it to take upwards of two or three weeks.

The Purpose of Live Rock

You may be asking yourself right now, what exactly does live rock do for your aquarium other than create a natural-looking reef structure? Just as live sand serves several purposes besides imparting a natural appearance, live rock does much more than provide a framework upon which corals can settle or attach.

Many of the same desirable organisms found in quality live sand are found in or on live rock, including a variety of diminutive worms, crustaceans, echinoderms, and mollusks. These organisms provide a readily available live food source for fish and certain corals. They're also fascinating to observe as they hatch out or emerge from various nooks and crannies and begin to proliferate in your mini-reef. I whiled away many hours during the setup phase of my mini-reef just marveling at the different life forms that seemed to appear spontaneously with every passing day–and that's before I'd even begun to add corals or fish!

Live rock comes in wide array of sizes and irregular shapes.

Macroalgae and calcareous coralline algae growing on live rock also serve important purposes apart from being attractive. A healthy crop of macroalgae, for instance, can help to keep nitrate, which it uses for food, to a minimum, thereby starving out hair algae and other undesirable forms of microalgae.

Encrusting coralline algae species, which look much like beautiful aquatic lichen, serve as good indicators of excellent water quality. In fact, in an aquarium where coralline algae are thriving, you can safely assume that most stony corals and other calcium-hungry reef invertebrates, such as the popular *Tridacna* clams, will too. A healthy growth of coralline algae will also inhibit the growth of undesirable algae species by out-competing them for substrate and nutrients.

Live rock is also a great contributor to the all-important process of biological filtration. Superior live rock, which is highly porous and convoluted, provides ample surface area for the colonization of aerobic nitrifying bacteria. Because of its porous nature, quality live rock also provides the appropriate oxygen gradient to allow for the growth of denitrifying bacteria deep within the rocks.

How Much Live Rock Do You Need?

I firmly believe that more is better when it comes to purchasing live rock. Most reef aquarium literature cites a stocking rate of 1 to 1 1/2 pounds of live rock per gallon of aquarium capacity. While this "rule" is certainly a good starting point, it doesn't take into account the variability of the weight-to-volume ratio that occurs from one type of live rock to the next. For example, 100 pounds of highly porous Fiji rock will likely fill up more space in your tank than will 100 pounds of aquacultured Florida live rock. It stands to reason, then, that the heavier the rock, the more you'll need to buy in order to create a naturalistic reef structure while still meeting the biological filtration needs of your aquarium.

Live rock affords the hobbyist many places upon which to set corals.

This End Up!

When placing live rock into the aquarium, the tank should be approximately half full with saltwater. Be careful not to fill it too much, or you'll end up with displaced water all over your floor–or, at the very least, you'll have to siphon out some of the water to accommodate all of your rock. Have more premixed saltwater handy so you can top off after adding the rock if necessary.

Also, keep in mind that each piece of live rock has an "up" side and a "down" side. That is, the side of the rock that was exposed to open water and sunlight in the ocean– which should be discernable by the greater abundance of life–should be oriented toward the surface of your aquarium. Naturally, then, the side that faced the sand should be oriented downward.

Aquascaping with Live Rock

The traditional approach to aquascaping with live rock is to build a pile that begins about 6 inches back (give or take) from the bottom of the front pane of the aquarium and rises gradually to a point just beneath the surface near the top of the back pane. The result is a uniform slope upon which corals are placed at varying levels, depending on their lighting requirements.

While this approach is certainly functional, it tends to lack something from the standpoint of aesthetics. The topography of natural coral reefs is irregular and multidimensional.

Thrusting peaks give way to plunging valleys. Massive outcroppings overhang mysterious caves. "Swim-throughs" connect one side of the reef to the other. Hardly sounds like the sloping monolith that was the mainstay of the mini-reef hobby for so many years, wouldn't you agree?

With a modicum of creativity, you can create a much more natural effect in your mini-reef. However, creative aquascaping with live rock does require considerably more planning. You might even want to draw a simple sketch of the desired result, or–if, like me, you have the artistic skills of the average four-year-old–you can refer instead to photographs of wild reefs for inspiration.

A power drill with a masonry bit can be your best friend when it comes to working with live rock. If your rockscape calls for two or more chunks of rock to be joined together–for instance, if you want to create a cave or overhang–you can simply drill appropriate holes using the masonry bit and fasten the rocks together with sturdy plastic tie-wraps. Don't worry about the tie-wraps showing. Before you know it, coralline algae will encrust any exposed plastic, effectively concealing it from view.

Creative aquascaping provides the basis for beautiful reef topography.

Aquarium-safe silicone sealant can also be used to secure rocks together so they won't topple over due to the machinations of fish and various motile invertebrates, or because of accidental avalanches caused by the aquarist during routine maintenance.

If you choose to secure your live rock reef structure with silicone, however, keep in mind that once the sealant sets up, the structure will be relatively permanent, and your freedom to change the rock configuration will become minimal. Careful forethought and planning will ensure that your live rock aquascaping is satisfactory to you and functional for the corals you intend to keep.

Uninvited Guests on Live Rock

While I'm singing the praises of the various beneficial encrusting organisms that are found on or in live rock, I should point out that there are certain undesirable ones–the uninvited live rock hitchhikers–that can find their way into your mini-reef as well.

Like weeds in a terrestrial garden, these undesirable organisms appear on live rock because they play an integral part in the complex web of life found on the coral reef. Just as the nefarious dandelion is perfectly adapted to thrive under less-than-ideal garden conditions, so too are these aquatic pests. And they can really wreak havoc once they come into their own within the confines of the

Mantis shrimps are capable of inflicting painful wounds to your fingers and hands.

mini-reef, where the absence of their natural predators allows them to multiply unchecked.

With Friends like These, Who Needs Anemones?

Aiptasia anemones (a.k.a. glass anemones or rock anemones) are among the more aggravating of the common live rock stowaways. These remarkably prolific creatures typically make their appearance shortly after live rock has been introduced to the aquarium. At first, just a few "cute" light brown to nearly transparent specimens crop up, and the unwary aquarist might even find them sort of appealing. But in no time, these seemingly innocuous anemones will reproduce to unmanageable proportions–and they make room for themselves in the mini-reef by stinging the heck out of any neighboring sessile invertebrates (i.e., your valuable corals and other invertebrates).

You can't simply pluck *Aiptasia* anemones from the rock to remove them from the system and then go on your merry way, either. In fact, attempting to destroy them by mechanical means, either by cutting them off at the base or crushing them, is an exercise in futility that only serves to create more *Aiptasia* because these pests can regenerate from even the tiniest remnant of tissue. If only it were that easy to keep clownfish host anemones alive!

Aiptasia anemones are harmful to your ornamental corals and invertebrates.

The key to controlling *Aiptasia* is early intervention. As soon as you observe a specimen, promptly remove the rock it's attached to from the system. If this is not possible, or if the anemones have already spread to neighboring rocks, more diabolical control methods may be called for.

You can attempt to eradicate *Aiptasia* by injecting each individual with a caustic chemical such as kalkwasser (a concentrated solution of calcium hydroxide) or sodium hydroxide (caution: highly caustic to the skin when concentrated). However, the injection method is painstaking, and you have to make sure you inject the chemical directly into the stem. Such precision is extremely difficult to verify, since *Aiptasia* tend to withdraw rapidly into miniscule holes in the rock when provoked.

A better option for controlling *Aiptasia*–albeit with some caveats–is to introduce one or more of its natural predators and let them do what comes naturally. The Peppermint Shrimp is one of several reef-safe species known to devour *Aiptasia*. However, it's very important to purchase the correct species (*Lysmata wurdemanni*), as several similar-looking species are sold under the common name "Peppermint Shrimp," but only *L. wurdemanni* is an effective *Aiptasia* eater. Ask for it by name!

Various butterflyfish, especially the Copperband Butterflyfish (*Chelmon rostratus*), are also known to eat *Aiptasia*. The drawback with this group of fish is that they may decide to sample your valuable corals and other invertebrates once they've eaten their fill of *Aiptasia*.

In recent years, an *Aiptasia*-nibbling nudibranch known scientifically as *Berghia verrucicornis* has found its way into the *Aiptasia*-control arsenal of many reef keepers. Some aquarists swear by this diminutive sea slug, while others have experienced mixed success with it. One drawback is the fact that *B. verrucicornis* is an obligate *Aiptasia* feeder, which means it won't eat anything else. Hence, after these nudibranches have done their dirty work, they must be removed from the aquarium or they will starve to death. Your dealer will, most likely, be glad to take them off your hands so he can resell them to another reef keeper.

Beware the Thumbsplitter!

The next live rock stowaway's nickname–thumbsplitter–should be enough to indicate that you might not want it in your mini-reef. I'm talking about the Mantis Shrimp. It gets this ominous nickname from fishermen and live rock collectors who have had the misfortune of being on the receiving end of its formidable hooked feeding appendages, or chelae, which can dispatch prey items and lay open fingers with a speed that is almost imperceptible to the human eye. Its common name, Mantis Shrimp, is based on its body plan and feeding technique, which are highly reminiscent of the praying mantis insect. Ironically, the Mantis Shrimp is not a shrimp at all, and is not even closely related.

Referred to as "thumbsplitters," mantis shrimps are one species that is best left out of the mini-reef.

Mantis Shrimps are stealthy nocturnal feeders that lie in wait with their lightning-quick chelae poised to lash out at passing fish and other invertebrates. Depending on the species, their chelae are adapted either to smash shelled prey or spear soft-bodied prey. Their powerful feeding appendages are even believed to have the strength to break the glass panes of aquariums! As you might imagine, a large Mantis Shrimp could do considerable damage to your valuable reef specimens within a short period, and you might not even detect its presence; you might simply notice that fish or prized invertebrates seem to be disappearing with no apparent cause.

I should clarify that there are many species of Mantis Shrimp, which vary considerably in size (anywhere from less than an inch to over a foot in length) and coloration, and not all are equally hazardous to aquarium denizens. In fact, they are often unjustly blamed for mysterious disappearances that may or may not have had anything to do with the Mantis Shrimp. Some aquarists are so enamored of the more colorful specimens that they'll even keep them intentionally–in single-specimen tanks, of course.

To catch a Mantis Shrimp, you can employ one of many commercially manufactured Mantis Shrimp traps, which are designed to be placed in the tank at night near the perpetrator's known or suspected burrow. Bait the trap with a little raw seafood, which the Mantis Shrimp should find irresistible, and you will eventually capture it. Some aquarists create Mantis Shrimp traps using sections of hamster maze baited with seafood. Whichever method you choose, should you find that one of these critters has made a home in your mini-reef, take considerable care when removing the trap, lest you become another victim of the thumbsplitter!

Some hobbyists actually keep these interesting creatures in single-specimen tanks.

Bristling Over Bristleworms

The last live rock hitchhikers we'll discuss are polychaete worms, known collectively as bristleworms. They are so named because of the rows of bristles lining their bodies, which are actually needlelike spines. When touched, these worms can produce skin reactions ranging from an itchy rash to a nasty burning sensation. The ones that cause a burning sensation, especially ones that happen to be red in color, are commonly known as "fireworms" in reef-keeper parlance. However, reefers are discovering that, while a few species (out of thousands) are destructive to reef invertebrates, most bristleworms are actually getting a bad rap.

When I first became interested in the reef-keeping hobby, bristleworms seemed to have a nasty reputation. Sensational accounts of fish being captured and devoured by bloodthirsty bristleworms frequently appeared in the aquarium literature of the time. Reef-keeper lore was fraught with tales of hobbyists being startled out of their sneakers by the sudden, unexpected appearance of enormous specimens.

Various crabs and other crustaceans often make their way into your mini-reef.

I even had such an experience myself a few years back. While quietly relaxing in my armchair in front of my mini-reef, the head of a copper-colored worm suddenly emerged from a hole in one of my live rocks. It began crawling across the substrate in the general direction of some dried nori (seaweed) I'd just put in the tank for my yellow tang. However, its tail end remained concealed within the rock. Like the pink bunny in that battery commercial, it just kept going and going and going. Approximately eight inches of worm emerged, yet I never actually saw the tail. The first thought that rushed through my brain was that I had to get rid of this intruder–and fast.

But you know what? I never quite got around to trapping that worm, and I have yet to observe any negative consequences from it. For all I know, the thing's probably still residing in my aquarium, bigger than ever, and feeding harmlessly on bits of nori and other detritus that settle into the substrate.

Where am I heading with this story and why am I sounding soft on bristleworms? Well, the truth of the matter is, with the exception of a few polyp-eating species, such as *Hermodice carunculata*, most bristleworms are completely benign in the aquarium. In fact,

Urchins can be exceedingly interesting to observe, but watch out for them while cleaning.

by consuming detritus, they play an important role as part of the aquarium cleanup crew.

Don't "bristle" too much about bristleworms unless you're faced with an especially large specimen that is causing noticeable problems. Oh, and if you happen upon one of these spiny fellows in your mini-reef, just keep your hands to yourself, and you won't have to worry about those venomous spines.

Should it become necessary to trap a large, troublesome specimen, there are plenty of commercially manufactured traps out there that you can try. Better yet, save yourself a little money by rigging a trap of your own. For instance, you can take a long glass tube, such as a pipette, and bait one end with a piece of raw seafood. Put your makeshift trap in the tank and check it several times after lights out. It may take a few tries, but persistence will eventually pay off.

Part Two

"Him? I wouldn't worry too much about him, buddy.
He does this every five minutes for attention."

6

Fill 'er Up!

The water surrounding natural coral reefs is remarkably pristine, with remarkably stable parameters. Your biggest challenge as a reef keeper–and I'm certain you're up to it–is to maintain outstanding water quality in the closed system of your aquarium over the life of your mini-reef, which I hope will be many, many years.

Water Quality Begins at the Tap

The challenge of providing the optimum water conditions that corals and other reef invertebrates demand begins with your tap water. In order to deliver the purest possible salt water to your corals, you must first find a way to eliminate the impurities that are present in even the most

A mini-reef such as this is the product of high-quality water and frequent partial water changes.

palatable tap water. You may not be aware of it, but the water from your tap most likely contains all kinds of contaminants that, while perfectly safe for us to drink, are deleterious to the health of reef invertebrates. These contaminants might include chlorine, chloramines, nitrate, phosphate, aluminum, copper, lead, and a host of other impurities.

So, if tap water is unsuitable for use in a mini-reef aquarium, aren't we defeated right from the start? Not if we first treat the water to remove (or significantly reduce) these impurities before mixing in the sea salt. This is best achieved with a reverse-osmosis filter, de-ionizing media, or for optimum results, a combination of the two.

What About A Reverse Osmosis Unit?

There are many brands of reverse osmosis (RO) units out there, but they all function in essentially the same manner. Water from your tap is forced under pressure through a semi-permeable membrane that removes most of the harmful contaminants. These contaminants are then carried away through the wastewater line to a nearby sink or floor drain. The RO membrane is rated according to how much purified water it can produce in a 24-hour period. That is why you will see them with numbers such as 50 gpd (gallons per day) attached to them.

Soft and stony corals alike will benefit from the use of RO water.

Why is it Called "Reverse" Osmosis?

In natural osmosis, water flows from an area of low dissolved solids to an area of high dissolved solids. Imagine two buckets of water connected by a tube at the bottom that has a semi-permeable membrane in the middle. One of the buckets contains saltwater (high dissolved solids) while the other contains freshwater (low dissolved solids). Over time, water will flow through the membrane from the bucket containing freshwater and into the bucket containing saltwater, raising the level in the saltwater bucket. With reverse osmosis, the pressure of the tap overcomes this natural osmotic pressure and forces the water through the membrane, effectively reversing the natural flow.

Depending on how many stages the unit has (some are two-stage, while others are three-stage), the water might pass through a sediment filter and a carbon block filter before actually entering the RO canister in order to maximize the life span of the delicate membrane. With RO/DI units, another canister containing a deionizing resin is added after the RO membrane. The DI resin chemically bonds with contaminants that remain in the RO-treated water, producing very pure water. Some reef aquarists dispense with RO altogether, opting instead to use only a DI unit for tap water purification.

One significant drawback to RO and RO/DI units is the large amount of wastewater they produce. However, resourceful and environmentally-conscious reef keepers have found a myriad of ways to put this water to good use, including watering the garden and houseplants. Also, creating RO water is an extremely time-consuming process, which is not surprising given the ratio of wastewater to pure water produced by many such systems–approximately 4:1 for one of the more efficient units.

RO or RO/DI purified tap water should be used whenever mixing saltwater for routine water changes and for topping off water lost to evaporation. Remember, when saltwater evaporates, the salt is left behind. Only pure freshwater (H_2O) actually evaporates. That means that you must routinely top off your mini-reef system with purified freshwater in order to maintain a stable salinity.

Is RO Really Necessary?

Some reef keepers boast success by using only a chemical dechlorinator as a tap water pretreatment instead of filtering their water by RO. However, only aquarists who are fortunate enough to have extraordinarily pure tap water can get by for long using this approach. I'd wager that those who claim success simply using dechlorinated tap water have likely not been in the hobby for long.

Heavy metals and other impurities commonly found in tap water tend to build up in the mini-reef system over time. You might notice no ill effects for several months but then gradually observe an inexplicable decline in the vitality of your corals and other invertebrates.

Fishes will also benefit from the pollutant-free water of an RO unit.

Also, many municipalities are not required by law to inform citizens beforehand when, for instance, there is a change in the municipal water purification protocol. In other words, merely using dechlorinated tap water is sort of like playing a game of aquatic Russian roulette. Why risk your precious corals just to save a few dollars in water-purification equipment?

Synthetic Sea Salt

Since you'll be going to all that trouble to purify your tap water via RO or RO/DI, it only makes sense to purchase a high-quality synthetic sea salt mix, too. Fortunately for modern reef aquarists, this is easy to do, since most reputable brand-name salt mixes are of very high quality. Some swear by one brand or another, but I've never noticed any appreciable difference from one to the next. Just be sure that the packaging on your salt mix clearly states that the product is free of nitrate and phosphate, both of which promote the growth of undesirable algae.

It hasn't always been so easy to lay your hands on quality synthetic salt mixes. In fact, the pioneers of our hobby had to either use natural seawater for their aquariums or–if you can imagine this–create their own salt mixes out of the various chemical components. Heck, I have enough trouble mixing up a batch of macaroni and cheese! And that comes with a recipe right on the box!

Going Natural

Speaking of natural seawater, shouldn't reef keepers living on the coast simply use the abundant natural resource that is so readily available rather than shell out the cash for a synthetic salt mix? While this is certainly an option, using natural seawater for a mini-reef has its limitations, especially for those of us who are landlocked.

For instance, just as with harvesting live sand, salt water collected too close to shore is very likely contaminated with a variety of pollutants, ranging from boat motor oil to sewage and even agricultural runoff. I certainly wouldn't recommend subjecting your valued invertebrates to such a chemical onslaught.

Water collected away from shore can be made suitable for aquarium use, but it requires some effort and patience. Natural seawater should be "aged" for approximately two weeks in a covered plastic container (any heavy-duty, food-grade plastic container is acceptable).

This waiting period ensures that any potentially troublesome planktonic organisms (living organisms suspended in the water) will die off and settle to the bottom of the container and will not enter your mini-reef system. Then you can siphon off the "clean" water, leaving behind any debris that settles to the bottom, and then add the water to your aquarium.

Regular partial water changes with RO water will make for a more stable environment.

I must say, though, that this sounds like a lot of needless effort to me—especially when synthetic sea salt mixes are so easy to use and so reasonably priced. I know that comments like this make natural-reef purists cringe, but I prefer the greater sense of control I get when I'm able to mix quality synthetic sea salt with purified tap water. That way, if I experience any water-quality problems later on, I can be fairly certain that the problem didn't originate with my source water.

Mixing it Up

We're almost ready to mix up saltwater and begin filling the tank. Of course, this step should be performed prior to adding any live sand or aquascaping with live rock. However, a non-live substrate can be added ahead of the water if you prefer. But if you've purified your tap water through RO or RO/DI, you'll need to attend to one more step before mixing it up.

Breathe New Life into Your Water

At this point, you should aerate the water vigorously for approximately 24 hours to replenish any dissolved oxygen that the water may be lacking. Vigorously aerating purified water also serves another important purpose. You see, RO/DI filters tend to do their job almost too well, stripping out virtually all of the dissolved minerals and producing product water that leans toward the soft, acidic side. Aeration helps to increase the alkalinity of the water—its ability to resist a change in pH in the presence of an acid—prior to mixing in the sea salt. Absent this step, the buffers present in the sea salt mix would be quickly used up, resulting in an unstable pH. Don't worry if terms such as alkalinity and pH are leaving you scratching your head right now. We'll cover them in much greater detail in the chapter on water parameters.

By the Tankful or by the Bucketful?

Mixing the synthetic sea salt with the purified water is a simple matter of pouring and stirring until the desired salinity level is reached. When first setting up a mini-reef system, and obviously before any aquatic organisms have been added, you can do the mixing in the tank itself. Simply fill the tank to the desired level with purified water and then begin adding the salt. If you're filling a large aquarium, you might want to place a powerhead into the tank to do the mixing for you. Keep in mind that you'll be adding live sand and a hefty amount of live rock, so you must allow for the displacement that will inevitably occur. Fill the tank only about one-half to two-thirds of the way with saltwater, depending on how light and porous your live rock will be, and mix up additional saltwater in a separate container so, if necessary, you can top off after the sand and rock are added.

Once your mini-reef is up and running and stocked with corals and fish, you'll need to mix your saltwater in a separate container. It should then be aerated overnight and heated to match the temperature of the aquarium water before you add it to the system.

Measuring Salinity

In aquarium literature, a commonly quoted acceptable range of salinity–measured as specific gravity (SG)–for the tropical marine aquarium is 1.022-1.024. I would suggest that, while marine fish can be kept at the lower end of this scale with no harm done, a specific gravity of 1.024, or even a bit higher, is recommended for corals and other sessile invertebrates.

Having said that, a greater concern than the exact specific gravity value in your mini-reef is the stability of the specific gravity value. While, in my humble opinion, corals are best kept in saltwater with a specific gravity of around 1.024 (or higher) on the aforementioned scale, they'll suffer considerably if that value is allowed to

Checking the specific gravity of your aquarium should be done on a regular basis.

fluctuate precipitously from one day to the next due to a poorly regulated freshwater top-off regimen. Your corals will be much better off if you select a specific gravity toward the higher end of the acceptable range and maintain it with minimal fluctuation.

Testing for salinity is accomplished using either a floating or swing-needle hydrometer. Both are inexpensive, accurate, and very easy to use. With the floating style, which is typically used in science and medicine, a float is spun in a glass cylinder filled with a sample of saltwater. The float, which is graduated, sinks to varying depths after spinning, depending on how much salt is dissolved in the water. To read the specific gravity, simply observe which value on the graduated float lines up with the surface of the water sample. You can also purchase floating hydrometers that are placed directly into the aquarium, although these models tend to be less precise than the other types.

Commonly available swing-needle hydrometers are even easier for aquarists to use. They also tend to be a bit easier to read without squinting. With this style, you simply fill the hydrometer with a sample of saltwater and observe how far the built-in swing-needle rises. Once it has stopped rising (actually, it typically bounces around a bit), it will point directly at the specific gravity value on a graduated scale that is imprinted on the side of the hydrometer itself. Who could ask for more?

Two types of high-quality hydrometers are shown here.

A hydrometer actually tests salinity indirectly by comparing the weight of a sample of saltwater (drawn from your aquarium) to the weight of an equal volume of distilled water. True salinity, on the other hand, is a measure of the total dissolved salts in a saltwater mixture, which is read in grams per liter or parts per thousand. For our purposes, though, measuring specific gravity will more than suffice.

Controlling the SG Ups and Downs

What happens if you're mixing saltwater, either in the tank during setup or in a separate container, and you accidentally add too much salt? Don't despair, because this is easy to correct! To my shame, I tend to get impatient with adding salt in small increments to reach the desired specific gravity, so I invariably go a little overboard on one of the last additions. But no harm done! All you have to do is add a little more freshwater to the mix to bring it back down.

However, adjusting the specific gravity in a stocked mini-reef demands a little more finesse. Remember, maintaining stability of all water parameters in a mini-reef is paramount, so adjustments should always be made as gradually as possible. This can be a challenge when the air humidity level is extremely low, causing evaporation to kick into high gear. Depending on the season and relative humidity, I might need to add anywhere from a quart to a full gallon of freshwater each day to top off my 75-gallon mini-reef.

Drip by Drip

Replenishing freshwater lost to evaporation is a daily chore that cannot be overlooked. As I touched upon earlier, routine freshwater top-offs are critical for maintaining a stable specific gravity in your mini-reef. Hence, it's imperative that you monitor the water level closely each day to determine how much purified freshwater needs to be added.

If your mini-reef system is equipped with a sump, that's the ideal place to monitor evaporation and to perform freshwater top-offs. And it won't be long before you're able to determine approximately how much water you need to add by just glancing at the water level in the sump or at the surface of your display tank, if no sump is used.

When topping off, it's a good idea to avoid dumping the entire quantity into the sump all at once. The return pump in your sump will immediately transfer that sudden influx of freshwater to the aquarium, bathing any invertebrates located near the outlet of the return hose with freshwater—not an ideal situation for most marine invertebrates!

A better approach is to top off over a longer period with some sort of drip system. This doesn't have to be anything complicated or costly. I use nothing more than an old one-gallon ice cream container with airline tubing and a plastic clamp from an enema kit. I drilled a small hole on the side of the container just above the bottom, inserted the tubing, and sealed it in place with aquarium-safe silicone. The clamp, which is located a few inches back from the end of the tubing, can be adjusted easily to control the flow rate so that the top-off water drips out very slowly, taking several hours to bring the water back to the desired level.

This is just one example of a simplistic drip system. Other automated freshwater top-off systems can be purchased or manufactured by the aquarist with a penchant for do-it-yourself projects.

Factors Influencing Evaporation

The daily top-off rate becomes rather predictable after a while, depending on various influencing factors. For example, I know that I'll need to add approximately one gallon of water to my 75-gallon system each day during our cold northwest Ohio winters, when humidity is extremely low. On the other hand, during our sweltering summers, when the air temperature is in the 90s and the relative humidity is approaching 100 percent, I know that I'll be adding approximately half a gallon a day, or even less.

Other factors that will influence the rate of evaporation in your mini-reef include:

• The intensity of the lighting you're using

• The presence or absence of a cooling fan (also dependent on the intensity of lighting you're using)

• The surface-to-water-volume ratio (how much of the aquarium's water is exposed to the air)

• The amount of water movement near the surface of the mini-reef

• The presence or absence of a wet/dry (a.k.a. trickle-down) filter system

Sinister Salt Creep and Specific Gravity

While evaporation and related factors tend to push specific gravity upward, there are influences at play that tend to push it downward, too. One of the biggest offenders is salt creep. No, salt creep isn't a sinister super villain (though it certainly sounds like one, doesn't it?). Rather, it's the salt buildup that gradually encrusts the rim of the tank, the light hood, power cords emerging from the display tank or sump, and just about any surface in close proximity to the aquarium. It's caused by the very fine spray that is inevitably produced by filter return hoses, powerheads, surge makers, or any device that agitates the surface of the water. Naturally, the amount of salt creep produced is directly proportional to the amount of surface agitation that is created.

Part 2

Show tanks need to be cleaned of salt creep on a regular basis.

Not only does sinister salt creep cause a gradual decrease in specific gravity, but if not cleaned frequently from power cords, it can also work its way down the cords until it eventually reaches the power outlet, causing an electrical short.

Salt creep is nearly impossible to stop, but it's relatively easy to clean up. Wherever possible, simply push the salt back into the aquarium or sump, taking care not to drop it directly on top of any corals or other invertebrates, as this will irritate their sensitive tissues. As a precaution against this, turn off any filters and powerheads ahead of time so that the salt chunks sink to the targeted area and do not drift onto your invertebrates under the influence of current. Power cords should be routinely wiped off with a slightly damp cloth.

What Else Lowers Specific Gravity?

Apart from salt creep, a small amount of saltwater is removed through the protein-skimming process each time the foam-collection cup is emptied. However, this has a negligible impact on specific gravity. A larger concern is performing haphazard water changes—e.g., mixing replacement water to a lower specific gravity than that of the aquarium, or removing more saltwater than is replaced and then making up the difference with freshwater.

Whatever the cause, if you should observe that the specific gravity in your mini-reef has dipped below the desired level, this problem should be corrected very gradually to avoid osmotic shock to your aquarium inhabitants. One way to achieve this is to perform several water changes over the course of several weeks, each time mixing replacement water that is slightly higher in specific gravity than the water in the mini-reef until the proper level is achieved. Or, each day for several days, dissolve a small amount of sea salt in a cup of aquarium water and very slowly pour it into the sump to correct the specific gravity.

Tropical Mini-Reefs Need Tropical Temperatures

Water temperature is one of many critical parameters in a mini-reef system that must be continually monitored and occasionally adjusted to maintain a stable value. What is the desired temperature range for the tropical mini-reef? This question brings us to the second major reef-keeping controversy that flares up from time to time. For the sake of amusement, we'll call this controversy the "Fantastic Fahrenheit Feud" (my apologies to readers who prefer Celsius).

Opinions Collide

If you can get three reef keepers to agree upon the same recommended water temperature for maintaining tropical sessile invertebrates, then a

Warmth and clarity are two important parameters in a mini-reef.

career in international diplomacy awaits you! One "expert" might argue–quite convincingly, too–that a water temperature range of 82° to 84°F is optimum for most tropical corals. Another "expert" might argue with equal conviction that the aforementioned "expert" is off his rocker and that corals should be kept in water no warmer than 75°F. Still another might split the difference and recommend a water temperature of 78°F.

The Ideal Temperature is Right in Range!

By now, you've probably figured out that a range of temperatures are acceptable for maintaining tropical reef invertebrates, and that there isn't necessarily one "right" answer to the question posed above. I would suggest that the optimum temperature range for most corals and other tropical sessile invertebrates is 75° to 80°F. Your corals and other invertebrates will adjust to any temperature within that range and thrive, provided the temperature remains stable. That means you'll need to take into consideration external factors that influence water temperature, such as summer highs, winter lows, whether or not your home is equipped with air conditioning, etc. when selecting a target water temperature.

Mushroom anemones are hardy and will commonly do well in a wide range of temperatures.

Your aquarium's lighting system might also have a considerable impact on your ability to maintain a stable water temperature. If, for example, you plan to illuminate your corals with high-intensity metal halide lamps, you'll almost certainly need to incorporate a small cooling fan in your lighting system to prevent temperature fluctuations from daytime to nighttime. On the other hand, if you choose to go with fluorescent lamps, which tend to run cooler, you might get by without the fan.

Monitoring and Adjusting Water Temperature

A water temperature check should be part of your daily maintenance routine, along with topping off freshwater, adding any necessary supplements, and evaluating the health of your specimens. Daily monitoring of water temperature might just save you hundreds of dollars in lost livestock in the event that the heater should fail, and this simple chore can be accomplished using one (or more) of a variety of inexpensive, aquarium-safe thermometers.

Thermometer Options

Nowadays, there's an aquarium thermometer to suit just about every taste and every pocketbook. For well under five dollars, you can choose from the following:

A floating thermometer with suction cups that can be attached to any smooth surface in your display tank or sump. Or you can dispense with the suction cups and simply allow the thermometer to float freely, but then it will tend to drift into hard-to-reach areas. I like to know right where to find my thermometer at all times, so I keep it contained inside my overflow box.

A standing thermometer, which has a weighted bottom so it can stand on the floor of the aquarium. Some aquarists like to use this style in conjunction with the floating style to get temperature readings at different depths.

A liquid-crystal stick-on thermometer, which is affixed to the outside glass of the aquarium. The advantages of this style are that you always know exactly where to find it and it will never develop that "lovely" coating of algae that sometimes makes in-tank thermometers difficult to read.

A floating dual-purpose thermometer/hydrometer–for those who like to check temperature and specific gravity at the same time.

Reefers with an affinity for the latest gadgetry (and who have a few extra dollars to spend) might prefer to use one of the newer remote digital sensor thermometers. This style comes with a probe that is placed in the water and a separate remote display unit that can be placed in a convenient location in the room outside the aquarium. Some of these units even come equipped with an alarm that will sound when the water temperature drops too low or climbs too high.

Aquarium Heaters

Fortunately for us modern reef keepers, today's aquarium heaters make water temperature

Aquarium heaters are simple to use and come in a wide array of sizes and wattages.

control a snap. Most styles today are fully submersible, so they can be placed conveniently out of sight down in the sump or craftily concealed within the rockwork in the display tank. Of course, the old-fashioned semi-submersible, hang-on-tank variety is still available, but apart from the slightly lower price tag, I don't see much benefit to them for mini-reef applications. After all, you're striving to create a naturalistic slice of coral reef, and these heaters are visually obtrusive, to say the least.

Modern submersible aquarium heaters are also simple to adjust. Most have easy-to-read temperature settings visible on the side or top of the heater, as well as a control knob on the top that allows you to adjust the heat output of the unit with degree-by-degree precision. The only drawback to submersible heaters is that if you opt to conceal them in the sump or rockwork, making simple temperature tweaks can become somewhat more of a challenge.

A welcome advance in submersible heater technology was the fairly recent introduction of unbreakable titanium thermometers. That's good news for aquarists who have experienced the heartbreak (not to mention the danger to life and limb!) of accidentally shattering a glass heater while rearranging live rock or performing routine maintenance chores.

Just as there are remote digital thermometer units, there are also aquarium heaters with separate computer controllers that allow aquarists to make any necessary temperature adjustments without getting their hands wet. Again, however, the more complex the heater, the more you can expect to shell out at the register.

How Much Wattage Should Your Heater Put Out?

Most aquarium heater manufacturers will indicate the size of aquarium that each unit is rated for on their product packaging. However, this can sometimes be difficult to ascertain. If you're not sure whether a particular heater has enough chutzpa to handle heating your mini-reef, here's a simple rule you can apply to find out: You'll need your heater to provide approximately 3 watts of heating capacity per gallon of aquarium water. For a 75-gallon aquarium, you'll need a heater that provides a minimum of 225 watts. (In all likelihood, you'll need to purchase a unit rated at 250 watts or greater, since I don't believe I've ever seen a 225-watt heater.)

But if a little wattage is good, isn't more wattage even better? Why not just drop the largest heater you can find into the tank and let it go to town? While this may sound like a good idea in theory, it's not such a good idea in practice. It's true that a 300-watt heater will bring your water to the desired temperature in half the time it takes a 150-watt heater, but that's precisely the problem–the temperature change takes place too quickly. When your mini-reef is fully stocked with precious corals and you observe a slight trend away from your target water temperature, you want the subsequent correction to occur very gradually. Remember, stability is an important key to success with mini-reefs.

What if the Heater Fails?

In years past, it wasn't uncommon to hear accounts of aquarium heaters failing in the "on" position and consequently cooking all of the aquarium inhabitants due to the precipitous rise in water temperature. Nowadays, heaters are designed to break in the "off" position, so the worst that happens is that the water temperature slowly drops until room temperature is reached. While a gradual drop to around 72°F might be stressful for tropical invertebrates, it certainly wouldn't lead to catastrophic loss of life–at least not in the amount of time it would take you to purchase a new heater (or better yet, hook up a spare one).

Many reef keepers prefer to use two heaters rated at a lower wattage rather than a single higher-wattage unit–e.g., two 100-watt heaters rather than a single 200-watt heater. That way, should one heater fail, the other will still put out heat, minimizing the impact on the aquarium's water temperature.

Just Chillin'

Okay, we've explored our choices for heating the mini-reef and the various thermometer options for monitoring water temperature. But what do you do if it's the middle of summer and excessively warm ambient air temperatures are causing your water temperature to rise beyond the acceptable range–and you don't have the luxury of air conditioning to help bring it back down? If you're facing this dilemma, you might want to consider investing in an electric chiller unit.

Aquarium chillers function in much the same way as a refrigerator or air-conditioning unit. Here's how they work: A refrigerant gas, such as Freon, is compressed, causing its temperature to drop. The refrigerant then travels to a heat exchanger, where it passes aquarium water that is being pumped from the tank and through the chiller. In the heat exchanger, heat is transferred from the water to the cold Freon. The water is then pumped back into the aquarium at the desired temperature.

While aquarium chillers are very reliable, accurate, and durable, they have one major drawback: They are prohibitively expensive for the average aquarist of modest means who has already invested a considerable sum just setting up a basic reef system. So how necessary are they?

I would argue that, under most circumstances, a chiller is not essential to success with a mini-reef. During many a late spring in northwest Ohio, when temperatures start to heat up but my wife and I are not quite ready to fire up the central air, I've anxiously watched my aquarium's water temperature creeping slowly upward to around 82°F and sometimes a bit higher. However, I've never observed any ill effects from this trend among my coral specimens. Of course, once the blistering heat of mid-summer arrives, the air goes on, and the water temperature returns to the desired range.

How to Beat the High Cost of Chillers

If soaring summer temperatures are inevitable in your area, air conditioning is unavailable, and a chiller unit is simply unaffordable, don't lose faith! Your mini-reef is still within reach. You'll just need to do a little extra planning to ensure the greatest amount of insulation from that blazing summer sun.

Start by positioning your tank in the coolest room in the house. A basement would be ideal, but I completely understand the desire to locate a mini-reef in a more prominent room in the house, where you can enjoy it as often as possible. If the basement is unacceptable (or there is no basement), place the tank in a well-ventilated ground-floor room out of direct sunlight. It's preferable to position the tank against an inside wall rather than an outside wall because an outside wall will tend to transfer outdoor heat to your mini-reef.

Next, provide as much air movement around the aquarium as possible to promote evaporative cooling. If you have a ceiling fan in the room, an attic fan in the attic, or both, keep them running when summer temperatures start to heat up. A small fan directed across the surface of the aquarium will also assist in evaporative cooling, and as mentioned earlier, may be necessary if metal halide lamps are used. As the name "evaporative cooling" suggests, you should be prepared to compensate for excessive evaporation by redoubling your freshwater top-off efforts.

Finally, choose a higher target water temperature, say 79° to 80°F, to maintain year round. This will minimize the potential temperature spikes on even the hottest days of summer.

Part 2

8

Shedding Light on the Subject

With the exception of certain specialized organisms that thrive near deep-sea thermal vents, virtually all life on earth depends to at least some extent on the power of the sun. Green plants use the sun's energy to carry out the all-important process of photosynthesis. Herbivores benefit directly from this process by browsing and grazing on green plants. Predators, in turn, consume the browsers and grazers, thereby benefiting indirectly from photosynthesis.

Light Support

It stands to reason, then, that sunlight also sustains life for many of the organisms found on tropical coral reefs. Because competition for

Zooxanthellae are responsible for the bright green color in these zoanthid polyps.

limited nutrients is so fierce among coral-reef denizens, many corals and other sessile invertebrates have evolved a very peculiar adaptation that allows them to use sunlight and the process of photosynthesis in order to thrive under such nutrient-poor conditions.

These so-called photosynthetic invertebrates, which include many soft corals, stony corals, giant clams, and anemones, harbor specialized symbiotic algae called zooxanthellae within their tissues. Not actually true algae, zooxanthellae are unicellular flagellates that use the power of the sun and the waste products of invertebrates to photosynthesize nutrients for survival. Any photosynthesized nutrients that the zooxanthellae don't use for themselves are shared with their invertebrate hosts–hence the symbiosis.

Great! But what does all this mean to the prospective reef keeper? Given the light-hungry nature of many of the invertebrates you might be considering for your first mini-reef, it's imperative to provide artificial lighting that is sufficiently intense and of the correct spectrum. In other words, you need your lighting to mimic the intensity and spectrum of the sun–to the extent that this is possible–with man-made lamps.

Appropriate artificial lighting ensures that the zooxanthellae continue to photosynthesize at the optimum rate and provide adequate supplemental nutrition to your invertebrates. Provide inadequate or inappropriate lighting, on the other hand, and your specimens will exhibit poor health and growth or worse yet, slowly waste away until they eventually perish. So, as you can see, a lot is riding on the quality of your mini-reef's lighting system!

The Trouble With Natural Sunlight

But if the purpose of your lighting system is to mimic natural sunlight for the benefit of your photosynthetic invertebrates, why not just use the real thing? Why not position your tank in front of a south- or west-facing picture window or beneath a skylight and let the sun illuminate your mini-reef? Indeed, some aquarium literature I've read recommends using natural sunlight for mini-reef illumination if possible, but I would suggest that this approach is fraught with limitations.

First of all, even the sunniest window exposure will only be sunny for part of the day. Factor in awnings, overhanging trees, and other obstructions, as well as the tangential angle at which sunlight enters a room through a window, and you'll soon realize how impractical and unmanageable this approach really is. A skylight presents even greater limitations. On its arc across the sky, the sun would shine directly down through the skylight and onto your mini-reef for a very short period indeed–certainly not long enough to sustain light-hungry invertebrates in good health for very long.

Second, excessive air temperature fluctuation is typical in the vicinity of windows and skylights, which will translate into water temperature fluctuations in your mini-reef–and there's not much you can do to prevent or control it, even if your home is equipped with central air.

Finally, from an aesthetic standpoint, it's extremely difficult to direct continually shifting natural sunlight onto a mini-reef aquarium in such a way that it is visually pleasing throughout the day. After all, most of us work during daylight hours, and I for one like to have the opportunity to relax in front of my mini-reef in the evening with my tank lights still turned on.

On average, hard corals need stronger lighting than most commonly available soft corals.

Artificial lighting, in stark contrast to natural lighting, affords the aquarist significantly greater control over the amount, intensity, spectral characteristics, and duration of illumination. Certainly high-intensity artificial lighting can generate heat sufficient to cause water temperature fluctuations, but it's relatively easy to counteract the heat generated by a light fixture that is isolated above your aquarium by installing a cooling fan.

Adrift in a Sea of Acronyms!

Getting a handle on all the mini-reef lighting options–not to mention understanding all the crazy lighting acronyms (HO, VHO, PC, MH, etc.)–can be a daunting task. But it's really not as complicated as it appears to be. Essentially, there are three general categories for mini-reef lighting: fluorescent, metal halide, and various combinations of the two. Granted, there are seemingly limitless options within these three categories when it comes to wattage, spectral characteristics, and configuration, but don't worry, we'll sift through the confusion in short order.

Don't Cut Corners With Reef Lighting!

Before we proceed too far down the road in our discussion about mini-reef lighting, I should bring one important consideration to your attention. For the average reef keeper, the lighting system will account for the single largest outlay of cash during the entire mini-reef setup process.

But the old adage "you get what you pay for" is axiomatic with reef lighting. It's very unwise to attempt to cut your overall setup costs by cutting corners with your lighting. If you do, I can almost guarantee that you (and your photosynthetic invertebrates) will be unhappy with the results, and, within a short time, you'll end up parting with even more cash to upgrade your lighting, anyway. You'll be better off in the end if you buy the best lighting system that you can reasonably afford right away. Believe me, if corals could talk, they'd thank you for making the investment!

How Much Wattage Will You Need?

Since light intensity (among many other factors) is such a critical consideration when choosing a mini-reef lighting system, it might be helpful to discuss the minimum light requirement for most photosynthetic invertebrates. But before we do, let me point out that the "rule" I'm about to introduce should be considered a very rudimentary guideline at best, which doesn't take into account factors such as the shape of the aquarium (length relative to height) and the varied illumination demands of coral reef invertebrates. However, I think it's important to have at least some point of reference so you don't end up purchasing a lighting system that is either grossly inadequate or total overkill.

For the sake of keeping it simple, let's assume that you should provide a minimum of 3-5 watts of light per gallon of aquarium capacity. A 55-gallon mini-reef would require a minimum of 165-275 watts, while a 75-gallon mini-reef would demand a minimum of 225-375 watts.

The Color of Light: Who's This Kelvin Guy, Anyway?

Along with wattage, aspiring reef aquarists must consider the spectral characteristics–or color–of light when choosing a mini-reef lighting system. As anyone who has ever experimented with a prism knows, sunlight is made up of many different colors, beginning with red and ending with violet. In between, you have orange, yellow, green, blue, and indigo. Colors toward the red end of the spectrum are filtered out at relatively shallow depths as sunlight passes through saltwater. Conversely, the colors toward the blue end of the spectrum penetrate much deeper. Hence, photosynthetic invertebrates derive the greatest benefit from lamps that radiate more of the deeper-penetrating blue end of the spectrum.

As you'll soon discover, reef lighting, whether fluorescent, power compact, or metal halide, will always have an associated Kelvin temperature rating; for example, 5,000 degrees Kelvin (5,000K). What does this mean? Kelvin temperature doesn't, as the name might imply, have anything to do with heat. Rather, it's a reference to the spectral characteristics of the lamp. Lamps with a higher Kelvin temperature rating radiate more of the blue,

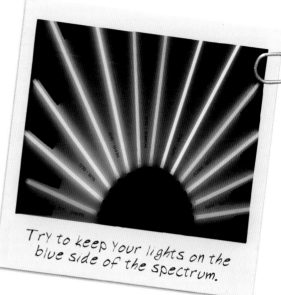

Try to keep your lights on the blue side of the spectrum.

violet, and greens of the color spectrum, while lamps on the lower end radiate more of the red, orange, and yellows.

Use lamps rated at 5,500K or higher to illuminate a mini-reef. The reason is simple: 5,500K is basically the Kelvin temperature rating of the noontime sun on a cloudless day. Also, lamps rated lower than 5,500K (such as many commonly sold horticultural "grow lamps") tend to promote the growth of undesirable algae.

Numerous lighting options and combinations are available for providing reef lighting of the appropriate intensity level and color spectrum. I suggest you speak to your local dealer, and together you should be able to come up with the perfect system for your mini-reef.

Photoperiod

Reef keepers also must address the issue of providing the correct photoperiod for their mini-reefs each day–in other words, leaving the lights on for the appropriate length of time each day so that the invertebrates receive an adequate period of illumination. For the tropical mini-reef, the optimum photoperiod is between 10 and 12 hours per day. There's no advantage to leaving the lights on longer, as this will only fuel the growth of problem algae.

These mushroom anemones appear to be reproducing and show good color—a sign of proper lighting.

Fluorescent tubes are by far the most common type of lighting used over mini-reef aquariums.

In order to provide a consistent photoperiod, I highly recommended using light timers to turn your lamps on and off at the same time each day. That way, variations in your work or social routines won't interfere with your lighting schedule.

For a natural sunrise/sunset effect, many reefers who have lighting systems that incorporate both daylight and actinic (blue) lamps time the actinic lamps to come on one or two hours before the daylight lamps and turn off one or two hours after. I don't know that this has any real benefit for the corals, but some say that the blue lighting allows the corals to adjust to the full intensity lighting coming on a short while later. The visual effect is also quite serene and calming, and the blue light makes the green pigments of some corals fluoresce in an almost otherworldly fashion.

Fluorescent Lighting Options

Aspiring reef aquarists often look first to fluorescent lights over metal halides because of their significantly lower price tag and convenience of use. Fluorescent lamps also produce significantly less heat than metal halides, which makes the use of cooling fans optional in fluorescent-only lighting systems. But where should one begin when shopping for fluorescent lamps? It's easy to get confused over all those acronyms—NO, HO, VHO, and PC. What exactly do they stand for, and how does each style differ from the other?

Normal Output (NO)

These are the standard 40-watt tubes typically used to illuminate fish-only aquariums, which do not require special, high-intensity lighting. Used alone, NO lamps are generally insufficient for meeting the lighting needs of photosynthetic invertebrates. However, as I'll explain shortly, NO tubes can perform an important aesthetic function in mini-reef lighting.

High-output (HO)

These tubes put out 65 watts per each 4-foot tube. This level of lighting is adequate for mushroom polyps and certain other soft corals that require only moderate light levels. However, because they are so limiting in terms of the photosynthetic species you can keep, most reef keepers overlook HO tubes in favor of VHO tubes.

Very High-output (VHO) and Power Compacts (PC)

VHO lamps provide 110 to 160 watts for, respectively, the 4-foot and 6-foot sizes.

PC, or power compact (you might also hear them called compact fluorescent), lamps provide lighting levels similar to VHO in a much smaller lamp and at much lower wattages. You can easily distinguish PC lamps from other fluorescent tubes by the fact that there is a plug (with either a square-pin or straight-pin configuration) at only one end of the lamp. PC lamps range in power output from around 9 watts (for nano-reefs) up to 96 watts. But again, you can't compare VHO and PC lamps on a watt-per-watt basis. For example, a 55-watt PC lamp is actually rated higher in output than a 110-watt VHO.

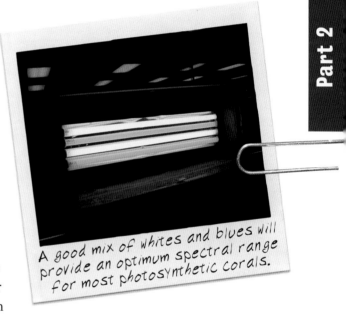

A good mix of whites and blues will provide an optimum spectral range for most photosynthetic corals.

Fluorescent Limitations

I'm a little reluctant to discuss this entire genre of reef lighting in terms of its limitations, since fluorescent lighting is so diverse and versatile, but there are a few drawbacks nonetheless.

While there are no hard-and-fast rules here, you can generally assume that fluorescent lamps, even VHO and PC, do not provide enough light intensity to adequately illuminate the lowest portions of deep aquariums–say, over 18 inches in depth. This is especially true

Here are two examples of waterproof end caps for fluorescent tubes.

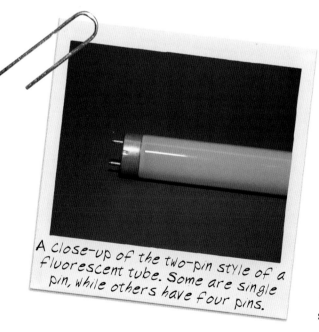

A close-up of the two-pin style of a fluorescent tube. Some are single pin, while others have four pins.

if the mini-reef is to be stocked primarily with small-polyped stony corals, *Tridacna* clams, anemones, and other invertebrates that usually require very intense lighting.

However, if a deeper mini-reef aquarium features mostly soft corals and perhaps a few large-polyped stony corals, which will thrive under moderate to bright lighting, then fluorescent lamps may very well be adequate.

Fluorescent lamps alone also tend to impart an unnatural floodlit look to the mini-reef–without the spectacular, eye-catching "glitter lines" that are produced on the coral reef through the interplay of sunlight and water motion. (To recreate this effect in the mini-reef, you'll need to employ metal halide lamps.)

Also, since fluorescent lamps cast light in 360 degrees, they must be installed beneath a highly polished metal reflector. Otherwise the light output that travels upward and to the sides is lost. A reflector captures most of this "misguided" light and directs it down on your mini-reef, where it belongs. Fortunately, most aquarium hoods already come equipped with reflectors, so this "drawback" is really not much of an issue unless you're planning a do-it-yourself lighting system. I should add that many light manufacturers now offer 180-degree lamps with reflectors built right into the fluorescent tube. Take care when installing these lamps, since there is a definite "up" side and "down" side.

Metal Halide Lamps

Metal halide lamps have become the workhorses of modern reef keepers' lighting systems and are recommended for deeper tanks (over 18 inches) and for shallower tanks housing small-polyped stony corals, *Tridacna clams*, and/or anemones.

Metal halides put out very bright lighting that brings us as close to the look and intensity of natural sunlight as modern technology allows. As I already mentioned, metal halide lamps are the only way, short of natural sunlight, to create those visually pleasing glitter lines. Not only are these glitter lines important from an aesthetic standpoint, but some studies suggest that they are also beneficial for the health of reef invertebrates. The theory is that this interplay of light and water movement actually intensifies the lighting with each ripple, which in turn stimulates the symbiotic zooxanthellae that reside in the tissues of light-hungry invertebrates to photosynthesize at the optimum rate.

Metal halide bulbs may be more costly to operate, but consider the expense a part of "doing business."

Commonly sold metal halide lamps come in 175 watts, 250 watts, and 400 watts. The appropriate wattage and number of metal halide lamps necessary for illuminating a particular mini-reef depend on several factors, including the depth of the tank and the invertebrates housed within it. To provide yet another somewhat overly simplified guideline, you should use 175-watt metal halide bulbs for tanks 18 inches deep or shallower, 250-watt bulbs for tanks that are 18-24 inches in depth, and 400-watt bulbs for tanks that exceed 24 inches in depth. Space the lamps out over the mini-reef so that there is one lamp for every two feet of aquarium length. For example, a 48-inch-long aquarium (a common length for 55- and 75-gallon tanks) would require two metal halide lamps for proper light distribution.

Metal Halide Drawbacks

Just as fluorescent lamps have their limitations, metal halide lamps have their own drawbacks to consider. The first drawback will be readily apparent when you start shopping for your lighting: Systems that include metal halide lamps are substantially more costly to purchase than most fluorescent-only systems. They're also somewhat more costly to operate, which may be reflected in your monthly electric bill. However, if your utility company allows you to make budgeted payments, this increase in power consumption is really not all that dramatic. Consider it part of the monthly cost of doing business.

As we've touched on already, metal halides–especially the higher-wattage bulbs–tend to generate much more heat during operation than fluorescent lamps do. This excess heat creates the potential for fluctuating water temperature. But again, the use of a small cooling fan (which will be included with most hood systems) should be adequate to counteract this problem. However, if your home lacks air conditioning and you intend to use 400-watt metal halides to illuminate your mini-reef, an electric chiller may very well become a necessity for you during the dog days of summer.

Your mother's advice about never looking into the sun also applies to metal halide lamps. Because metal halides are point sources of intensely bright light, they can damage your vision and should never be viewed directly. While this isn't such a serious concern when the lamps are mounted in a hood that rests directly on top of the tank, it can be a real problem with pendant-style fixtures that are suspended above the aquarium.

The Best of Both Worlds

Up until now, we've been discussing mini-reef lighting options as being separate from one another, but most reef aquarists illuminate their mini-reefs using a combination of lamp styles. A typical combo includes both daylight and actinic lamps, which can be created using metal halide/fluorescent, metal halide/PC, PC/PC, or fluorescent/fluorescent combinations.

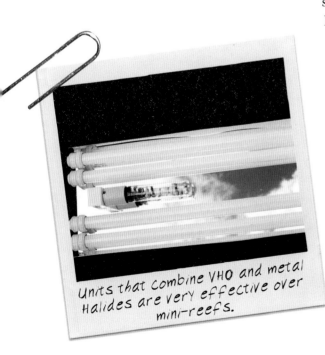

Units that combine VHO and metal Halides are very effective over mini-reefs.

For instance, to illuminate my 75-gallon mini-reef, I currently use a combo hood that is outfitted with two 175-watt, 10,000K metal halide lamps, and two normal-output actinic fluorescent tubes. The metal halides alone provide sufficient light intensity for the photosynthetic corals in my care, but I chose to include the normal output actinic tubes simply because, when combined with the metal halides, they impart a more natural look–albeit slightly more bluish than might suit some aquarists.

But my approach is only one potential lighting combination. Some reef keepers prefer to use metal halide lamps with a lower Kelvin temperature rating, say around 5,500K to 6,500K, supplemented with VHO or PC actinic tubes to create the look of a sun-drenched shallow reef setting.

The possibilities are virtually endless! Can't find a particular lighting combination in a ready-made hood? There are also myriad ways to do it yourself when it comes to mini-reef lighting. Don't care for the lighting combination in the hood you've got? Then purchase a retrofit kit and swap out the lights that you find disagreeable. Can't decide which combination of lighting to choose? Ask your dealer for suggestions, or visit a reef keepers' forum and ask for input there.

Where Should You Stow the Ballast?

High-intensity lighting, whether metal halide or fluorescent, necessitates the use of special ballasts (transformers) that produce lots of heat (unless you use electric ones) and, when combined with salt water, pose the risk of electric shock. These factors should dictate how and where the ballasts are positioned. To play it safe, stow your ballasts in a well-ventilated area away from flammable materials–but not in a cabinet-style aquarium stand–where they cannot be affected by the occasional saltwater spill. Of course, you should protect all of your aquarium's electrical equipment, including the lights, with a ground-fault circuit interrupter (GFCI), which will disrupt the flow of electricity in the event that any energized equipment is accidentally immersed.

More Is Not Necessarily Better!

One very common misconception about mini-reef lighting is, if a certain level of illumination is good, much, much more must be even better! While one could argue that it would be hard to overilluminate a mini-reef stocked primarily with SPS corals (small-polyped stony corals) or *Tridacna* clams, the same cannot be said for a mini-reef stocked mostly with soft corals.

In fact, it's entirely possible to provide too much light for some soft corals, which they will manifest by refusing to open up, by attempting to relocate

Small shelves enclosed in the aquarium's canopy are ideal spots for stowing timers and dimmers.

themselves to a less intensely lit area, or worst of all, by perishing. For example, mushroom polyps and related corals, many of which hail from deeper waters, tend to fare quite poorly under intense metal halide lighting. I've even observed mushroom corals under such circumstances attempt to escape the intense light by dividing or detaching and "dripping" down from the main colony onto lower rocks or down to the substrate where the light level is more subdued.

It's imperative to match the output of your lighting with the needs of your invertebrates, and there is no one-size-fits-all mini-reef lighting system. Keep this in mind when you're selecting your livestock. As much as possible, try to limit your invertebrate purchases to species that occupy the same niche on the reef, so you won't end up trying to satisfy wildly disparate lighting needs with one system.

Part Three

"Francis, who are we kidding! There's no way we're going to get clean in this place! We're just soaking in our own filth"

Water Purification

Perfectly translucent saltwater–you know, the kind of clarity that makes fish appear to be floating in midair– is a hallmark of a well-maintained mini-reef. But this level of clarity is not achieved by accident. Rather, it results from ongoing, disciplined attention to proper water purification techniques on the part of the reef keeper.

We've already discussed the importance of treating your tap water via RO, DI, or RO/DI, but that's only a small part of the water-purification picture. Aquarium filtration in all its forms, a process called protein skimming, and routine water changes fill in the rest of the picture.

Wave action is the ocean's version of protein skimming.

Fine filtration media is great for polishing the water before it's returned to the tank.

Some hobbyists prefer to use a coarser grade of media than the white type pictured above.

In this chapter, we'll cover the different types of filtration and the importance of protein skimming. In the next few chapters, we'll get into water changes and some optional water-purification tools that you might eventually consider adding to your arsenal.

Mechanical Filtration

When most people think of aquarium filtration, the first thing that comes to mind is the form commonly known as mechanical filtration. With this form of filtration, aquarium water passes through some sort of filter medium (e.g., foam sponge, spun-nylon floss, fiber pad, etc.) that strains out fish poop, uneaten food, and other particulate matter suspended in the water. Mechanical filtration is the most basic form and the easiest for most people to comprehend, since they can actually observe the process (i.e., water passing through a medium) and the result (i.e., a dirty filter medium).

If you've kept a fish-only aquarium of any kind, then you're probably quite familiar with the process of mechanical filtration and the devices that are used to provide it. Indeed, in the marine fish-only aquarium, the use of fairly powerful mechanical filters–typically canister filters or hang-on-tank filters–is recommended to keep pace with the heavy waste output produced by a community of fish as well as the uneaten food particles that inevitably result from overzealous feeding.

But in the mini-reef, the role of mechanical filtration isn't quite as clearly delineated. Nowadays, more and more reef keepers are getting away from powered heavy-duty canister or hang-on-tank filters, relying instead on more passive methods of mechanical filtration, such as placing a prefilter sponge in the overflow chamber that leads down to

Part 3

the sump. The reef keeper must routinely rinse the sponge to remove particulate matter from the system before it decomposes and releases nitrogenous waste into the water. Gently vacuuming the substrate with a siphon during routine water changes is another method that helps to keep particulate waste and the nasty byproducts of its decomposition under control.

Biological Filtration

If you remember our earlier discussion of the nitrogen cycle, then you should already have a pretty good grasp on the process of biological filtration. To reiterate briefly, ammonia produced by decomposing organic material is acted upon by one group of aerobic nitrifying bacteria, which produces nitrite. Another group of nitrifying bacteria convert the nitrite to nitrate, which is then either removed from the system through partial water changes or converted to free nitrogen and oxygen gases by denitrifying bacteria that reside deep within the substrate or live rock.

Bioballs provide a good medium on which beneficial bacteria may grow and colonize.

No other process occurring within an aquarium is more important than what I have just described, and certainly, no animals should be added to your mini-reef before testing indicates that biological filtration is ongoing and the aquarium is considered completely "cycled." So how do you go about getting this cycle started in your mini-reef?

Don't Doom Damsels!

For many years, it was common practice among aquarists to introduce damselfish to newly set up marine tanks in order to jumpstart the cycling process. These rugged little fish would provide "food" for the beneficial nitrifying

Years ago, we used damsels to "jumpstart" our biological filtration.

Part 3

bacteria in the form of their waste products. Being amazingly resilient, the damsels would usually survive the progressive assaults of ammonia and nitrite, which would likely kill more sensitive species in short order.

However, this approach certainly cannot be recommended for, and should not be adopted by, today's conscientious reef aquarist. The most obvious prohibition against using damsels for cycling is the fact that, no matter how you look at it, it's inhumane to subject a living thing to such abuses. Sure, damsels might survive under these poor conditions, but at what cost to their overall health? After all, a person could probably survive spending a week in a portable restroom that is in need of emptying, but it certainly wouldn't be a healthy experience! Besides, there's more than one way to cycle a mini-reef!

Let Live Rock Handle the Load—Bioload, That Is!

With live rock in ubiquitous use among reef keepers, there's absolutely no need to subject damsels to the rigors of the cycling process. Live rock offers ample surface area for the colonization of nitrifying bacteria, and the additional die-off that invariably occurs on newly acquired live rock will provide more than enough dissolved organic waste to feed nitrifying bacteria.

Live rock offers ample surface area for the colonization of beneficial bacteria.

While live rock should never be added to an established mini-reef before it has completely cured (lest you risk causing a potentially lethal ammonia spike), there's no reason you can't take advantage of this additional die-off period to cycle your new mini-reef before adding any livestock.

And that's precisely how I prefer to cycle a mini-reef. After cleaning as much debris and decay from the rocks as I can, I stack them in the aquarium (which is half filled with saltwater) in the desired configuration, top off the tank with saltwater if necessary, and let the cycling begin!

When cycling with live rock, I make sure that the lighting, water purification, and heating equipment are all properly tweaked and in full operation, just as they will be when the

Part 3

invertebrates are added, so that the surviving encrusting organisms have a chance to adapt to normal operating conditions. However, some aquarists disagree with this approach, preferring to keep the lights off to discourage the proliferation of troublesome algae.

Monitoring the cycling process involves regular testing with ammonia, nitrite, and nitrate test kits. You should first observe a spike in the ammonia level followed by a drop in ammonia and a spike in nitrite. Once nitrite drops to the point where it is undetectable, nitrate will begin to accumulate. At this point, you should perform a partial water change to lower the nitrate level to zero and voila, your mini-reef is completely cycled! Depending upon how much additional die-off occurs, cycling with live rock should take somewhere near ten days to two weeks.

The Trouble with Trickle Down

While live rock provides ample capacity for biological filtration in a mini-reef aquarium, some reef keepers prefer to hedge their bets by including a wet-dry, or trickle-down, biofilter in their setups as well. This brings us to the third major controversy among reef keepers: the biofilter battle.

Before I delve into the controversy of using a wet-dry biofilter in a mini-reef setup, it might be helpful to describe exactly what a wet-dry biofilter system is. Many versions of these systems are on the market, but they all work in essentially the same manner.

One popular design works like this: Water from the display tank passes into a slotted overflow box located inside the tank near the surface of the water. A U-shaped siphon tube draws the water from the inside overflow box to another box that hangs on the outside of the tank. A prefilter sponge may be located in this external box to keep detritus from entering the biofilter. From there under the influence of gravity, the water flows downward through a flexible tube to the

This trickle filter is quite advanced compared to many that are commonly available.

Part 3

biofilter chamber, where it trickles over some form of biofilter medium, such as a sponge, grooved plastic spheres, porous ceramic blocks, or spun nylon floss.

The biofilter chamber itself is positioned in the sump just above the water level, so the filter medium is never fully submerged–hence the "dry" part of the name. The water trickling over the porous filter medium keeps it constantly moist and highly oxygenated, providing the ideal breeding ground for nitrifying bacteria. The beneficial bacteria do their work, converting ammonia to nitrite and nitrite to nitrate, and then the water is pumped back through a return hose to the display tank.

Sounds like wet-dry systems do a great job of biofiltration, right? So why all the controversy over using them to filter mini-reefs? Well, the problem is, they tend to do their job too well. In other words, they're highly efficient at producing the result of nitrification–nitrate– which, as we've already established, is harmful to sessile reef invertebrates even at low levels. To further complicate matters, wet-dry filters are not conducive to the colonization of denitrifying bacteria, which are needed to convert nitrate to free nitrogen gas.

It's this very reason that many reef keepers prefer to forgo the use of wet-dry systems, relying solely on live rock to tackle the chore of biofiltration. But don't the nitrifying bacteria colonizing the live rock produce nitrate as well? Indeed they do, but the difference is, the nitrate is produced in close proximity to denitrifying bacteria that reside slightly deeper in the rocks. Therefore, the nitrate is promptly converted to nitrogen gas before it has a chance to diffuse throughout the aquarium–or so the theory goes, anyway.

So, does this mean I'm saying that you shouldn't include a wet-dry filter in your mini-reef setup? No, not necessarily. As long as you are aware of the system's limitations and take appropriate steps to prevent the buildup of nitrate, there's no reason you can't take advantage of the extremely efficient nitrification it provides.

Chemical Filtration

Chemical filtration in the mini-reef, if employed at all, typically involves the use of activated carbon to remove dissolved pollutants from the aquarium water through adsorption–not to be confused with absorption, as with a sponge.

Activated carbon is produced by baking a material like wood or coal at extremely high temperatures. Baking opens up tiny pores on the surface of the material and chemically alters the substance so that it tends to attract the molecules of various dissolved compounds.

For use in the aquarium, activated carbon is typically placed within a flow-through pouch of some kind so that the diminutive particles aren't scattered throughout the system. An old nylon stocking is just perfect for this purpose, provided it doesn't have too many holes or runs in it. The pouch is then inserted somewhere in the aquarium system, such as down in the sump or in an overflow chamber, where the water will continuously run through the activated carbon. As the water flows through the myriad tiny pores, dissolved compounds bond chemically with the surface of the carbon and are removed from the water.

Some filtration units have chemical modules that can be added or taken away depending on the application.

Activated carbon can be very useful in the mini-reef when it comes to removing harmful dissolved compounds, including the toxins that many corals, sponges, and other sessile invertebrates release in an effort to inhibit neighboring corals from infringing on their territory. However, it is indiscriminate in the dissolved compounds it adsorbs, so desirable substances, including many aquarium additives and trace elements, may get removed as well.

Being highly porous, activated carbon is also conducive to the colonization of nitrifying bacteria. That would seem like a good thing, but since carbon must be changed out on a regular basis, a portion of your system's biological filtration capacity is lost with each change. In addition, if activated carbon is left in your aquarium too long after it is completely used up, adsorbed pollutants can begin to leach back into the system because the carbon is beginning to break apart. You can circumvent both of these problems somewhat by keeping three or four pouches of carbon in your mini-reef system at one time and rotating one out with a fresh pouch about once every couple of weeks.

Part 3

Yet another drawback to the use of activated carbon is that certain low-grade carbons will leach phosphate into the water. Unless you're fascinated by the growth habits of troublesome algae species, this is very undesirable in the mini-reef. Be sure to use only products that are clearly labeled as phosphate-free.

Besides activated carbon, there are various resins and granular filter media designed to target particular dissolved substances, such as phosphate, nitrate, ammonia, and silicate, which can be used in the mini-reef if necessary. However, the appearance of one or more of these dissolved substances most likely indicates a larger problem with your maintenance methodology that must be addressed before it threatens the health of your livestock.

The Protein Skimmer

Although the protein skimmer doesn't fit neatly into any one of the filtration categories described above, I believe it is indispensable to providing outstanding water quality in the mini-reef and therefore belongs in the same chapter as the other basic filtration techniques.

Protein skimmers are perhaps the best way to remove pollutants from your aquarium's water—next to water changes, of course!

For proponents of the so-called Berlin method of reef keeping, which is based on a style developed in Germany back in the 1970s, the protein skimmer is the backbone of the water purification system. No other man-made filtration devices are included with this approach, and the critical processes of nitrification and denitrification are provided through the copious use of live rock. Many modern reefers enjoy considerable success using the Berlin method, which is, I believe, a testament to the efficacy of the protein skimmer.

Protein skimming mimics a natural process that you may have observed at the seashore while watching heavy surf crash onto the beach. I'm referring to the foam that is left behind as each wave retreats. This foam is produced when tiny bubbles of air, which are trapped by the crashing waves, combine with molecules of dissolved organic compounds in the water.

To clarify how this process is replicated with a protein skimmer, let's examine how one of these devices actually works. A small water pump attached to the skimmer pushes aquarium water into a tall, transparent reaction chamber. Simultaneously, air is injected into the chamber, forming thousands of extremely fine bubbles that rise up through the water. The molecules of dissolved organic compounds are considered bipolar. That is, one end is attracted to water (hydrophilic) while the other end is attracted to air (hydrophobic). As the bubbles rise, dissolved pollutants adhere to the surface of the bubbles and are carried up to the collection cup at the top of the chamber. There, they form thick, brown foam, which eventually collapses into a foul-smelling liquid. The aquarist then empties the collection cup, thereby completely removing the pollutants from the system before they can decompose and further burden the biofilter.

Protein skimmers also alleviate the effects of "coral chemical warfare" on the mini-reef inhabitants. As you may or may not be aware, corals and other sessile reef invertebrates (not to mention certain macroalgae) are a toxic lot, releasing all kinds of nasty chemicals into the water to keep competition for valuable reef real estate in check. While there's no test kit that reef keepers can use to verify the presence of these chemicals, you can sometimes tell (or at least suspect) they are there when various corals in the mini-reef refuse to expand and no other cause can be determined. Aggressive protein skimming will minimize the presence of these chemicals and by extension, minimize the amount of time your inverts remain inexplicably contracted.

Some Skimmers are Better By Design

While all protein skimmers essentially operate on the same principle, there is some diversity in design that can influence the effectiveness of these devices. One important difference relates to the direction of water flow in the reaction chamber. With so-called countercurrent skimmers, the water enters the chamber through slots at the top and flows down in the opposite direction of the rising bubbles. This

Small hang-on skimmers are perfect for small aquariums.

design results in optimum skimmer efficiency because it provides the maximum amount of contact time between the air and water.

The method by which air is injected into the reaction chamber can also affect the efficiency of protein skimmer operation. For instance, some models rely on air pumped through limewood airstones to produce a stream of bubbles that rises through the chamber in a linear fashion, while others utilize a venturi valve to produce a mixture of water and air in a whirling vortex of bubbles.

In my opinion, the venturi-driven models are far superior to airstone-driven models when it comes to producing bubbles of the appropriate size and quantity, as well as providing optimum air/water contact time. Also, with venturi-driven models, you don't have to worry about replacing clogged airstones every month or so. From my standpoint, the only drawback to venturi-driven skimmers is that, with some models, the air intake occasionally becomes clogged with salt and calcium deposits. However, this is easily remedied by briefly soaking the clogged component in a little white vinegar.

Dry foam that is full of air bubbles indicates that your skimmer is working properly.

You Can Judge a Skimmer by its Foam

One nice thing about protein skimmers is that you can readily determine whether they're making a difference in your water quality by simply looking at the amount and quality of foam they produce. A well-designed, properly functioning skimmer will produce copious amounts of very thick, dry, brown foam, which slowly collapses into a dark brown liquid. On the other hand, a skimmer that produces nothing but transparent to tea-colored water is either a mediocre skimmer or in need of adjustment.

If the skimmer worked well at one time, producing foam of the appropriate quantity and consistency, but is beginning to produce mostly water, you can safely assume that more air needs to be mixed with the water. On occasion, I'll notice this change start to occur with my venturi skimmer, so the first thing I check is the air intake, which I will usually find to be clogged with calcium and/or salt. Again, however, after a few minutes soaking the part in vinegar, my skimmer is back in business, skimming away at peak efficiency! If you're using an airstone-driven skimmer, excessive water production usually indicates that the limewood airstone is clogged and needs to be replaced.

Skimmer Styles

Protein skimmers are available in many different styles, ranging from compact models that hang on or in the aquarium to tall columnar models that are designed to be freestanding or placed down in the sump. Some styles even combine protein skimming and biological filtration technology in a single unit. The style that is best for you depends on a number of factors, including the size of your mini-reef, the amount of livestock you plan to include, how natural you'd like your mini-reef to appear, and so on.

Each skimmer style is usually available in a range of sizes as well, based on the aquarium capacity they're rated for. For instance, one skimmer style might be available in three different sizes—one for a 55-gallon tank, a slightly larger version for a 75-gallon tank, and an even larger version for a 100-gallon tank. Many reef keepers recommend purchasing a skimmer that is one size larger than needed; for example, using a skimmer rated for a 100-gallon tank on a 75-gallon tank. Since under-skimming is a more likely problem than over-skimming for novice reef keepers, I would tend to agree with this one-size-larger suggestion.

Part 3

Water Changes—The Reef Keeper's Best Friend

Allow me to begin this chapter by making the following bold claim: Virtually any water-quality problem you might encounter as a reef keeper will be improved to at least some degree by performing a partial water change.

Water changes dilute dissolved pollutants and help to replenish essential trace elements that have been used up by the tank's inhabitants. But what is most fascinating about water changes is the almost immediate positive effect they seem to have on fish and sessile invertebrates. Every living thing in the mini-reef seems energized by the influx of clean saltwater, which isn't surprising when you consider that natural reefs are essentially in a

Small-polyped stony corals like this Acropora need strong current and very clean water to thrive.

constant state of water change due to ever-shifting currents and wave action.

Ironically, in the early days of the reef-keeping hobby (before high-quality synthetic sea salt was made available), water changes were performed rarely, if at all. "Old salts" would even boast about how much time had passed in between water changes. But knowing what we know now about the importance of water changes—and with inexpensive synthetic salt mixes so readily available—we modern reefers have no excuse except our own laziness for postponing water changes.

How Much and How Often?

The first questions most newcomers to the mini-reef hobby ask about water changes are, "How much should I change?" and "How often should I change it?" In general, I would say that the ideal regimen is to make small water changes on a frequent basis. To elaborate further, I would recommend changing approximately ten percent of your mini-reef's water about once every two weeks. Better yet, make a five-percent change every week—or even smaller changes more often than that.

But why not just change 20 percent about once a month? After all, won't you end up changing the same quantity of water? Besides, you'll waste a lot less time on water changes if you perform one big change instead of several small ones over the course of a month, right? Both good points, but they overlook one of the basic tenets of reef keeping: Maintaining stable water parameters is paramount for successful husbandry of sessile marine invertebrates. Large water changes carried out infrequently equal greater fluctuations in pH, alkalinity, calcium level, trace element levels, and other important water parameters. Frequent small changes, on the other hand, make a negligible impact on the stability of these parameters but still manage to reduce the harmful nitrogenous compounds.

A bucket and a siphon tube are the telltale tools of the trade when it comes to water changes.

I should point out that changing 20 percent of your mini-reef's water volume will suffice if you have a low to moderate bioload (the amount of organisms in your mini-reef). If you have a heavy bioload, on the other hand, you might need to make larger changes. Testing for the presence of nitrate, phosphate, and other testable dissolved pollutants will help you tailor your water changes to meet the demands of your particular system.

Preparing the Replacement Water

Preparations for a partial water change in a mini-reef aquarium should begin at least two days in advance. On the first day, you'll need to produce the required amount of RO-purified tap water, which can be quite a time-consuming process in itself, depending on how much is required. As you'll recall from chapter 6, before mixing in the sea salt, the RO-purified water must first be aerated vigorously overnight to increase the pH and dissolved oxygen level. The next day, you can go ahead and mix in your sea salt to the desired specific gravity (1.024).

Water changes are a must in "frag" tanks.

Before using your new batch of replacement saltwater in your mini-reef, though, you'll need to make certain that the salt has had a chance to dissolve and mix completely and that it is the same temperature as the water in your aquarium. To accomplish this, place a small submersible aquarium heater and a small recirculating pump into the mixing vessel and allow the saltwater to sit covered for another day or until it's reached the appropriate temperature.

Also, make sure that the container you use for mixing saltwater is made of plastic or some other reef-safe material–never metal. Five-gallon food-grade plastic buckets are perfect for this purpose, and many restaurant operators are more than willing to part with them if asked. Of course, you can always use the large plastic buckets that sea salt is sold in as well.

Time for a Change!

Once your replacement water is completely mixed and heated to the correct temperature, you're ready to perform your water change. But first, double check the specific gravity to make sure the reading hasn't changed from its earlier value. Sometimes you'll notice a

Part 3

Of course, the diligent care that is offered to your corals will certainly benefit your fishes as well.

slight shift in SG after the salt has been given time to dissolve completely. Make small SG adjustments as necessary by adding more salt or more RO-purified water.

Next, shut off your filtration system and any powerheads that might become exposed to air as the water level in the tank goes down. If you have any corals or other invertebrates that cannot tolerate exposure to air positioned at the highest level of the rockwork, you might want to move them down to the substrate temporarily while you complete the water change. This would apply to many large-polyp stony corals, such as bubble corals (*Plerogyra* spp.), open brain corals (*Trachyphyllia* spp.), and elegance corals (*Catalaphyllia* spp.), which are very fleshy species that will likely sustain tissue damage if not fully supported by water. (Incidentally, these corals really don't belong high up on the rockwork, anyway, but that's a topic for a later chapter.)

Finally, before you begin siphoning out water, do any necessary glass scraping to remove algae that might be obscuring your view of the mini-reef. The same applies to any excessive algae or detritus that's growing or building up on the rocks. Gently brush algae off the rocks with a soft-bristled brush and dislodge detritus with a carefully directed blast from a turkey baster or powerhead. That way, the algae and detritus will be loose and free-floating, so you can easily vacuum them up with the siphon and remove them from the system.

For the next step, you'll need a siphon hose with a vacuum attachment at the end and a large plastic bucket to catch the wastewater. Please do not use your mouth to start the siphon! Not only is this unnecessary, but it's also objectionable when you consider all the dissolved pollutants in the water. Take a look at the gunk accumulating in your protein skimmer's collection cup and you'll get the idea!

To start the siphon flowing, simply lower the vacuum end of the hose into the aquarium with the open end facing up. Place the other end of the hose into the wastewater bucket. Once the vacuum end fills with water, slowly raise it up out of the aquarium so that the water begins to flow down into the bucket. Before the vacuum end empties completely, lower it back down into the water until it is fully submerged again. If you do it right (it may take a little practice), the water should continue to flow through the hose and down into the bucket. To break the siphon, simply lift the vacuum end out of the water with the open end facing down.

Once you've got the siphon flowing, begin to vacuum up any detritus or algae that you dislodged earlier. However, if your mini-reef has a DSB, take great care not to disturb it with the vacuum. Otherwise, you risk sucking up large quantities of the sugar-fine sand, along with any sand-stirring organisms residing in it.

Siphon out no more wastewater than you can replace with your pre-mixed, clean saltwater. When you've drained enough out, break the siphon and set the hose aside. But don't dump your wastewater down the drain just yet! Leave it in the bucket and use it to rinse out sponges or other filter media that might have become clogged with detritus.

Once this chore is accomplished, go ahead and dump the water, but as you do, keep an eye out for any diminutive invertebrates that might have gotten sucked up accidentally by the siphon, such as brittle stars and amphipods. More than likely, you'll find them crawling through the gunk on the bottom of the bucket. These should be slurped up with an eyedropper and released back into the aquarium to help maintain the desirable microfauna in your system.

Any plankton-eating fish in your mini-reef will benefit from this step in the water-change process. My Royal Gramma (*Gramma loreto*) seems to derive considerable amusement from dashing out of his tiny cave and gobbling up the amphipods before they reach the bottom of the tank. This is also the only time I can ever observe my secretive Mandarinfish (*Synchiropus splendidus*) actually eating something! I can't deny that it's fun for me to watch this natural feeding behavior.

Other Cleaning Chores

After you've finished your water change and the water is back to its original level, you can go ahead and restart your filter pumps and powerheads. At this point, you might also want to attend to a few additional cleanup chores.

Part 3

Scraping your aquarium's glass on a regular basis will prevent unsightly buildup from occurring.

For instance, you should empty and rinse out the collection cup from your protein skimmer. You may need to use a brush on the inside of the cup to dislodge the sticky gunk that has adhered to the sides and bottom. You should also clean the inside "neck" of your protein skimmer's reaction chamber, which will also be coated with sticky gunk, by wiping it with a moist towel.

Next, clean off any salt creep that has built up on the top edge of your aquarium, your lighting system's cover glass, power cords, and any other surface within reach of salt spray. As you do this, look over all of your aquarium components—pumps, heater, lights, ballasts, etc.—to ensure everything is connected and functioning properly and for evidence of corrosion or excessive wear. Promptly replace any components that give cause for concern. Better to spend a few dollars to replace a suspicious component now than to lose all of your priceless invertebrates later due to catastrophic equipment failure!

Finally, devote a little hard work to cleaning the outside glass of your mini-reef, which most likely has had saltwater splashed and dripped upon it during the course of your water change. Avoid using any chemical cleansers—especially those administered via aerosol or pump sprayer—which can drift into your aquarium, to the detriment of your invertebrates and fish. Instead, simply moisten a towel with tap water, wipe the glass clean, and then dry with a separate towel.

Water Purification Bells and Whistles

Several ancillary water-purification devices have come in and out of vogue among reef keepers in recent years. We'll call them the "bells and whistles" of water purification, since they certainly aren't critical for success with a mini-reef. However, if used properly, each can play an important role in bringing out the best in your mini-reef's water quality.

Should Your Reef Catch Some Rays?

One of these items is the ultraviolet (UV) sterilizer. Briefly, a UV sterilizer is an ultraviolet fluorescent bulb mounted in a watertight tubular chamber. Depending on the size of aquarium the sterilizer is rated for, the wattage of the UV bulb can range from 4 watts up to 50 watts or even more.

Sun corals not only need clean water but plenty of food as well.

It's important for your equipment to function as well as it looks.

However, for the average aquarium–say somewhere in between 55 and 100 gallons–a 9-watt UV sterilizer will probably suffice.

These devices work by pumping water from the aquarium through the sterilizer's chamber and past the bulb at a very slow flow rate, which irradiates the water, killing waterborne bacteria, viruses, algae, fungi, and parasites by altering their DNA. By decimating these free-floating organisms, the aquarist hopes to eliminate the potential for disease outbreaks and troublesome algae.

Depending on the manufacturer, the water flows around the bulb in various patterns–spiral, helix, etc.–in order to maximize exposure time between the water and bulb. The longer the water is exposed to the UV rays, the more efficiently these devices eradicate all of the aforementioned microscopic organisms.

There are two commonly sold styles of UV sterilizer on the market, one style being significantly more costly than the other. Why the cost difference? With one style, nothing stands between the bulb and the water, so to speak. That is, the bulb, while watertight, actually has water flowing over its surface. As you might imagine, the non-insulated style poses a greater risk of electric shock in the event that the bulb housing becomes cracked or compromised. Also, the bulbs in these units tend to become coated with slime rather quickly, reducing their overall effectiveness.

With the second, more expensive, style, the ultraviolet bulb is contained within a protective quartz sleeve, which is desirable not only from the standpoint of safety, but because the protective sleeve also prolongs the efficient lifespan of the bulb by preventing the aforementioned buildup of slime, although the quartz sleeve can now be covered by such a slime. As a result, some types of UV sterilizers now have a device that allows hobbyists to wipe off the slime. These units work well and greatly enhance the effectiveness of the UV sterilizer.

So, what's the consensus among reef keepers about the value of using UV sterilizers for mini-reef applications? Well, as with so many aspects of reef keeping, there is no consensus about UV sterilizers. Opponents of their use point out the fact that UV sterilizers kill all microfauna that pass through them, including larvae and other organisms that serve as important food sources for the invertebrates. Proponents of UV sterilizers, on the other hand, believe that the loss of some beneficial organisms is an acceptable tradeoff for the health benefits these units provide.

In the Ozone

Another ancillary water-purification device that some reef aquarists swear by and others swear at is the ozone generator. Ozone (O_3) is a naturally occurring gas that, if applied properly in the mini-reef, can have a positive impact on the system's water quality. However, if ozone is misapplied, the consequences to your livestock can be very serious indeed–hence the disagreement on its use in the mini-reef.

On the upside, ozone oxidizes dissolved organic compounds, increases the dissolved oxygen and redox levels (don't worry, more on this in the chapter about water parameters), increases the efficiency of protein skimming, kills germs, and improves water clarity.

Great, so what's all this about "serious consequences if misapplied"? Well, if excessive ozone is accidentally released into the aquarium water, it can, quite frankly, wipe out all your livestock. Therefore, the reaction between ozone and aquarium water is necessarily confined to a reaction chamber–usually the protein skimmer, though you can also purchase a dedicated reaction chamber.

Here's how the process works: Ozone is produced inside the ozone generator when air is brought into contact with a special UV light. The air is either forced into the generator with a pump or drawn in by a venturi valve. The ozone is then injected into the protein skimmer, where it reacts with aquarium water

A tangle of wires and hoses is a common sight behind many advanced reefers' aquariums.

inside the skimmer chamber. The ozone-treated water flowing out of the skimmer must be chemically filtered through activated carbon to remove any traces of ozone before it returns to the mini-reef. Also, since high concentrations of ozone in the air can be harmful to people, air escaping into the room from the reaction chamber must be either filtered through activated carbon or vented to the outdoors.

Controlling the amount of ozone used is where many reef keepers get themselves into trouble. Due to the incredible diversity of stocking rates and maintenance practices, there's no simple formula that will bring about the desired results in all reef aquariums. Therefore, the level of ozone is best controlled with a redox potential controller.

As I mentioned, ozone increases the redox–or oxidation-reduction–potential of the aquarium water. By using an electronic redox controller in conjunction with your ozone generator, you can easily regulate the amount of ozone produced so that the desired redox level, within 350-400 millivolts, is constantly maintained.

I should also point out that ozone tends to break down plastics and certain other materials, so all system components that will come into contact with ozone, including the protein skimmer and the tube connecting the generator output to the skimmer input, must be constructed of ozone-resistant materials. Your dealer can help you in regard to selecting appropriate ozone-resistant products.

Algae That Earns its Keep

A third ancillary water purification device (actually more of a system) is the algae turf scrubber, or ATS. With this type of system, troublesome algae growing in the mini-reef display tank is starved out by, well, other algae. Sound bizarre? Allow me to explain.

An ATS system is a shallow tank, separate from the display tank, that contains plastic screens upon which various turf-type microalgae are grown. Water is pumped from the main tank into the ATS tank, where it trickles slowly over the algae-laden screens. As you already know, algae uses nitrate, phosphate, and other dissolved pollutants as a food source. Hence, these compounds are taken up from the aquarium water by the various turf algae in the ATS before it is pumped back into the display tank. Periodically, the aquarist removes one of the screens and scrapes off the algae, effectively exporting the pollutants from the mini-reef system. The scraped screen is then recolonized by algae from the adjacent screens. So, theoretically, once the turf algae in the ATS take up any dissolved pollutants and the algae are harvested, no dissolved pollutants are left in the water to sustain irksome algae growing in the display tank.

Of course, algae needs light as well as dissolved nutrients to grow, so ATS tanks must be illuminated with intense lighting. Light is usually provided on a reverse-daylight cycle, which simply means that the ATS lights are on when the mini-reef lights are off, and vice versa. The two lighting systems should not be kept on simultaneously or you risk causing dramatic fluctuations in the pH and dissolved oxygen levels from day to night.

Another benefit of the ATS tank is that, over time, it becomes a safe refuge–or refugium– for various tiny organisms and larvae. As these organisms proliferate, some are invariably swept into the display tank, where they become food for hungry fish and invertebrates. Purist ATS users scorn the use of protein skimmers in their systems because they tend to skim out many of these beneficial organisms.

Algae turf scrubbers have their bad points as well as their benefits. As you might imagine, it's not completely unheard of for the cultivated turf algae species to find their way into the display tank. Also, the algae tend to promote yellow water, especially in systems where protein skimmers and/or activated carbon are not used. Not only is this yellowing unsightly, but it also reduces the amount of light that reaches photosynthetic invertebrates.

Final Thoughts on Bells and Whistles

Would I recommend using a UV sterilizer, ozonizer, or algae turf scrubber? As I mentioned at the beginning of this chapter, I don't think they're absolutely essential for success with a mini-reef. However, I wouldn't discourage their use, either, because what works for one reef keeper may be of no practical use to another. Remember, there's no right way to set up a mini-reef. We each have to make equipment decisions based on the characteristics of our own unique systems and personal experiences.

There, how's that for a copout?

Part 3

Mini-Reef Water Parameters

You've probably noticed that I've mentioned the importance of maintaining stable water parameters in a mini-reef several times now without getting into a detailed explanation of exactly what these parameters are and how to go about maintaining them. This chapter is devoted to demystifying mini-reef water parameters–such as calcium level, alkalinity, pH, carbonate hardness, redox potential, and dissolved oxygen–and the methods used to maintain them for those readers who, like me, find chemistry somewhat baffling.

Calcium in Mini-Reefs

Stony corals use it to make their skeletons. Soft corals use it to make the specialized sclerites that

Specialized aquariums need to have their water parameters monitored closely.

give them structure and support to their otherwise flaccid bodies. Crustaceans and echinoderms use it to make their rigid exoskeletons. Mollusks use it to make their protective shells. Tubeworms use it to make their tubes. Virtually all marine organisms depend on it to some extent for proper development. What is this all-important element? I'm talking about calcium, without which no mini-reef could thrive.

In natural seawater, calcium is present at a level of approximately 420ppm (parts per million). The level you should strive to maintain in your mini-reef is between 400 and 450ppm (some calcium hardness test kits give measurements in milligrams per liter, which roughly translates to parts per million).

In the closed system of the mini-reef, calcium gradually becomes depleted as the various organisms extract it to satisfy their growth requirements. The rate at which this depletion occurs can vary considerably depending on the type of invertebrates you keep. For instance, a mini-reef system containing all stony corals and perhaps a few *Tridacna* clams will become depleted much more rapidly than will a system housing only soft corals. Therefore, no simple formula can determine exactly how much calcium to add each day per gallon of system water.

Tridacna clams require a high concentration of dissolved calcium in their water.

The aquarist should do some cautious experimentation to determine exactly how much of a particular calcium additive is necessary to maintain the desired level of 400-450ppm. Of course, this experimentation must be coordinated with frequent testing, using a high-quality calcium hardness test kit. Dosing calcium additives in a haphazard fashion without careful monitoring will not only throw your calcium level out of whack, but it will also disrupt the delicate balance of interdependent water parameters, such as alkalinity and pH.

Supplementing Calcium

So, what methods can mini-reef aquarists employ to maintain calcium at the appropriate level? Actually, there are several acceptable calcium-supplementation methods you can use, each of which has its good and bad points. You may need to try each technique, or a combination of techniques, until you settle on the method that works best for your particular system.

Liquid Calcium

Let's start with the supplementation method that is the simplest and least demanding of your time–liquid calcium. With this method, calcium in liquid form–usually calcium chloride–is administered to the aquarium each day at the manufacturer's recommended rate (for example, 1/4 to 1 teaspoon each day per 50 gallons of aquarium capacity).

Pretty straightforward, right? Well, yes and no. While liquid calcium is very easy to dose, you can't use it by itself without upsetting the delicate balance among calcium, alkalinity, and pH. You must, therefore, use a buffering product in conjunction with liquid calcium so that your alkalinity level won't take a precipitous plunge and take the pH level down with it.

Two-part calcium/alkalinity additives, which are designed to be added to the mini-reef in equal parts, are available from several manufacturers. These two-part systems are sold in both ready-to-use and concentrated formulas. Buying the concentrated form is considerably more cost-effective because, in essence, you're not paying to ship as much water as you are with the ready-to-use formula. Besides, to make the concentrated additive ready-to-use, all you have to do is mix it with the recommended amount of purified tap water.

While two-part additives are very simple to use and, hence, very desirable for those of us with hectic schedules, they run out quickly and must be frequently replaced.

Kalkwasser

A tried-and-true additive that supplements both calcium and alkalinity in the mini-reef is kalkwasser, or limewater. Kalkwasser is a saturated solution of calcium hydroxide that is made by mixing 1 to 3 teaspoons of calcium hydroxide (recommendations vary considerably) with a gallon of RO-purified water in a durable plastic or glass container that can be tightly capped. The mixture is then covered and allowed to sit for several hours (often overnight) so that any powder that does not remain in solution will settle to the bottom of the container. The clear to slightly milky water above this layer of settled powder is then decanted from the mixing container and dripped very slowly into the mini-reef.

Part 3

Kalkwasser is commonly used to replenish lost calcium in aquariums containing stony corals.

A slow drip rate is critical because kalkwasser has a very high pH (upwards of 12) and will cause an unacceptable rise in your aquarium's pH if administered too quickly. Some aquarists purchase dosing systems that are specifically designed to administer kalkwasser at the correct rate.

Of course, as with virtually all aspects of reef keeping, there's a labor-saving gadget you can purchase–this one's called a kalkwasser reactor, and it automates the addition of kalkwasser. These "kalk reactors" produce a continuous supply of supersaturated calcium hydroxide and use a stirring mechanism, either a powerhead or a magnetic stirrer, to automatically mix the calcium hydroxide powder with purified water. These units are usually placed in line between the sump and a holding tank that contains RO- or RO/DI-purified freshwater. A float valve is used in the sump so that top-offs occur automatically whenever the water level in the sump drops below a certain point.

Kalkwasser can be used for all of your daily freshwater top-offs, or if your system's calcium demand is lower, you might want to space the doses out to every other day or so. Mix no more kalkwasser than you can use up in approximately one week. And remember, calcium supplementation must always be coordinated with routine calcium hardness testing, using a high-quality test kit.

The Calcium Reactor

Another device that can be used to supplement calcium and alkalinity is the calcium reactor–not to be confused with the kalkwasser reactor. A calcium reactor is basically a reaction chamber filled with some form of calcium carbonate medium, such as aragonite. As water from the aquarium flows into the chamber, carbon dioxide gas is simultaneously injected. A bubble counter is used to monitor and control the amount of carbon dioxide entering the chamber. The carbon dioxide lowers the pH inside the chamber to around 6.5 or so, which dissolves the calcium carbonate medium, releasing calcium and bolstering the alkalinity level.

A calcium reactor that has been properly assembled and "tweaked" is a very reliable technique used for maintaining calcium and alkalinity. However, the initial outlay of cash–for the reactor and carbon dioxide cylinder–might be prohibitive for some. That being said, the ongoing costs associated with calcium reactor use aren't exceptional relative to other calcium supplementation methods.

Resisting Change: The Role of Alkalinity

Alkalinity is a term that causes considerable confusion among novice reef keepers–probably because it is so often used interchangeably with other terms such as "buffering capacity" and "carbonate hardness." Well, let's see if we can shed a little light on these confusing terms.

For our purposes, alkalinity can be defined as the ability of a solution to resist a downward change in pH in the presence of an acid. In the mini-reef, the aforementioned "solution" is simply the aquarium water. The "ability to resist a change in pH" is just a fancy way of saying buffering capacity. And the "acid" is introduced via the natural biological processes–such as nitrification and metabolism–that are going on in the aquarium.

So, if the buffering capacity of the mini-reef is too weak to neutralize all the acids being introduced–for example, if the system is overstocked, overfed, or both–the pH will eventually start to fall below the acceptable level.

To help visualize this relationship, try to remember the last time you got carried away eating spicy Mexican food and had to chew antacid tablets later to soothe your ailing stomach. In this scenario, the spicy food represents the acid attempting to drive down pH, and the antacid tablets represent your system's buffering capacity.

So, how does carbonate hardness fit into this picture? Well, an aquarium system's alkalinity, or buffering capacity, is determined primarily by its carbonate hardness level–the amount of carbonates and bicarbonates present in the water. Hence, most commonly sold alkalinity test kits on the market actually measure carbonate hardness and express the results in degrees of German hardness, or dKH. Some test kits, however, give results in milliquivalents per liter, or meq/l (1meq/l = 2.8dKH). Other non-carbonates contribute to total alkalinity as well, but since carbonates make up approximately 96% of the alkalinity picture, measuring carbonate hardness gives us a fairly clear idea of a system's buffering capacity.

Part 3

Proper alkalinity will often allow enhanced coralline algae growth.

Supplementing Alkalinity

As I mentioned earlier, alkalinity is usually supplemented simultaneously with calcium by adding a buffering compound in conjunction with liquid calcium, by using two-part calcium/alkalinity supplements, by dripping kalkwasser, by using a calcium reactor, or by combining various supplementation techniques. Synthetic sea salt mixes contain buffers in correct proportions, so each time you do a water change, you're also helping to restore alkalinity. Whichever method or combination of methods you use, maintain your system's alkalinity at a stable level within the range of 7-10dKH (2.5-3.5meq/l).

When supplementing alkalinity and calcium, it's important to understand that these two parameters are closely interrelated such that one level cannot be altered substantially without impacting the level of the other.

For example, let's imagine that testing indicates your mini reef's alkalinity has dropped slightly below the desired minimum level of 7dKH but your calcium level is at the maximum desirable level of 450ppm. Should you simply keep adding larger and larger quantities of buffer to the system until the KH level is back where it belongs? Unfortunately, the solution's not that simple–the reason being, well, the solution. You see, there's a limit to the amount of solids that seawater can hold in solution. Therefore, attempting to "drive up" one level will tend to cause a downward trend in the other. So, in the scenario described above, dramatically increasing the amount of buffer added to the system would most likely cause calcium to suddenly precipitate out of solution, which is a highly undesirable result. You're better off maintaining a stable calcium/alkalinity balance, even if one value is slightly lower than desired, rather than dosing excessively and indiscriminately with calcium or buffers.

Understanding pH Without a Ph.D.

As it relates to aquarium systems, pH can be defined as a logarithmic measure of hydrogen ion concentration in an aqueous solution.

Yeah, it's Greek to me, too! Since the goal of this book is to keep things simple (thankfully!), let's define pH as a measure of how acidic or alkaline your aquarium's water is on a scale from 0-14–with 7 being neutral, any value below 7 being acidic, and any value above 7 being alkaline. Incidentally, "alkaline" in this context refers to pH values that are more "base," or less acidic, not to buffering capacity. In the mini-reef aquarium, a stable, slightly alkaline pH in the range of 8.2-8.4 is desired.

The natural proclivity of pH in the closed aquarium system is to trend downwards over time. This is due to several natural factors that gradually diminish the system's buffering capacity. For example, nitrification and the respiration and metabolic processes of marine organisms produce acids that deplete buffers. Also, reef invertebrates extract buffers (i.e., carbonates) from the water to aid in the production of their calcareous skeletons, shells, or exoskeletons.

Algae in a mini-reef system–whether desirable, cultivated macroalgae or invasive microalgae–will cause a slight decrease in pH over the course of the day, measurable after "lights out." This is due to the natural photosynthetic activity of the algae and is nothing to be alarmed about. When the lights are on, green algae take up carbon dioxide and produce oxygen. But when the lights are turned out and photosynthesis ceases, the algae take up oxygen and produce carbon dioxide. Being acidic, carbon dioxide contributes to the depletion of buffers and therefore lowers the water's pH.

Problems with plummeting pH can also often be attributed to improper husbandry and maintenance practices on the part of the aquarist. Testing for pH in a mini-reef that is overstocked, overfed, and neglected in terms of water changes and other routine maintenance chores will likely reveal dramatic, unacceptable fluctuations in pH value. Insufficiently aerated systems also tend to suffer pH swings due to the buildup of carbon dioxide in areas with poor water movement and inadequate gas exchange. It should stand to reason, then, that a mini-reef system that is judiciously stocked, impeccably maintained, and well aerated should experience minimal pH swings.

Redox Potential and Dissolved Oxygen

Redox potential and dissolved oxygen are two important water parameters that aquarists often overlook. While I don't believe that an in-depth understanding of these two parameters is essential to success with a mini-reef, they warrant a brief mention here simply because I think it's important to have at least some knowledge of all the factors influencing the health and well-being of your livestock.

Reading Up on Redox

The redox potential, or oxidation-reduction potential, of aquarium water is a reliable indicator of its quality and suitability for sustaining reef organisms. While recommendations for the desired redox potential in a mini-reef vary considerably, a value that falls somewhere between 350 and 400 millivolts (mV) should suffice for most reef invertebrates and fish.

Redox levels remain high in systems where dissolved organic pollutants, which degrade water quality and deplete the oxygen necessary for respiration and other important processes, are present in minimal (read: safe) concentrations. Conversely, redox measurements below the acceptable range indicate deteriorating water quality and should prompt corrective action. I should clarify, however, that as with most water parameters in the mini-reef, the stability of redox potential is of greater importance than the exact value. So, if your system's redox value consistently measures slightly below the desired range but your livestock appear perfectly healthy (and all other parameters check out okay), there's no compelling reason to alter your techniques.

As I mentioned in the previous chapter, the use of ozone is one way to ensure that your aquarium's redox potential remains sufficiently high. However, if you'd rather not fool with ozone, performing frequent partial water changes, maximizing aeration, and practicing sound stocking and feeding practices are also surefire ways to bolster redox potential.

Deep Breathing

Anyone who has observed the powerful surge action, currents, and tides associated with coral reefs should understand that dissolved oxygen plays a vital role in the health of corals, fish, and other reef organisms. On natural reefs, all of this dynamic water movement continually traps air, causing dissolved oxygen levels to approach, or even exceed, saturation. In the mini-reef, however, oxygen super-saturation is nearly impossible to replicate and therefore represents a very unrealistic goal. A more attainable dissolved oxygen level–and one your invertebrates and fish can certainly live with–is between 6 and 7ppm.

So how do you go about providing the appropriate level of dissolved oxygen for your mini-reef? If dynamic water movement is what promotes oxygen saturation on the coral reefs, it behooves us to provide as much water movement in the mini-reef system as technology allows.

The brisk aeration that a protein skimmer provides is one step in the right direction. I know that trickle-down biofilters have their detractors, but these controversial systems are quite superb when it comes increasing dissolved oxygen levels. If you simply can't abide incorporating biofiltration other than that provided by live rock and/or a DSB, consider removing the biomedia from the trickle-down and using the system for oxygenation purposes only. Powerheads and filter return hoses that are positioned so they agitate the surface of the aquarium are also helpful when it comes to increasing dissolved oxygen levels.

Mini-Reef Additives and Test Kits

Look over the shelves of your local reef aquarium dealer and you'll be amazed at the diversity of additives and supplements available to reef keepers today. We've already discussed some of the additives used for maintaining calcium and alkalinity levels, but what about all those other chemicals, trace elements, and formulations on the market–iodine, strontium, molybdenum, magnesium, iron, manganese, and vitamin supplements.

The chemicals and trace elements sold in various formulations by reef aquarium dealers do play an important role in the health of mini-reef organisms. In fact, all are present–and in the correct proportions–in high-quality synthetic sea

Aquariums containing many corals will require frequent testing and supplementation.

salt mixes. But using commercial additives is not always the most efficient way to introduce many of these important elements to your aquarium.

A major concern associated with using some mini-reef additives is that there are often no readily available corresponding test kits for monitoring the elements these additives contain. Without the ability to monitor the levels of common non-testable elements, and with only the manufacturer's recommended dosing rate as a guide, the aquarist has virtually no assurance against underdosing or overdosing. In such cases, it is best to use these with caution and awareness.

After you've spent even a short amount of time in the mini-reef hobby, you will undoubtedly hear or read that iodine additions have a marked impact on soft coral growth and are needed to stimulate the pulsing action of pulsing *Xenia* corals. However, an overdose of iodine can have profoundly adverse effects on an otherwise healthy complement of coral reef organisms. If you choose to supplement iodine, or any other non-testable trace element, be certain to follow the manufacturer's dosing instructions. If a range of dosing levels is included in the label instructions–for example, "add 1/4 -1 tsp per 55 gallons of aquarium capacity" (or some such)–always start with the lowest possible dosing level and work up gradually as needed.

Are You Making Chemical Soup?

When I first dove into the reef-keeping hobby, I was most decidedly guilty of the dash-of-this-and-dash-of-that approach to aquarium additives. I figured that if all of those elements are present in natural seawater, then it certainly couldn't hurt to buy a bottle of each and dose it on a regular basis. However, it didn't take me long to realize the error of my thinking. Even though I was dosing my mini-reef with every trace element known to man, my corals never seemed quite contented with the situation. In fact, they seemed rather irritated and often refused to open up for days at a time. But what else did I expect? I was creating a virtual chemical soup of trace elements, not one of which was likely in correct proportion–and certainly nothing close to the natural composition of seawater!

Remember, our overriding goal as reefers is to provide water conditions that are both stable and as close in composition to natural seawater as current technology allows. At the very least, haphazard dosing of aquarium additives--even if well intentioned--will prevent

Part 3

you from achieving this goal. In a worst-case scenario, it might even cause the demise of your valued invertebrates.

Synthetic Sea Salt: Everything in Proper Proportion

As I've already hinted, the best method for replenishing non-testable chemicals and trace elements extracted from the water by reef invertebrates is to perform frequent partial water changes using purified tap water and a high-quality synthetic sea salt mix. Everything you need to promote a healthy reef is right there in the salt mix—and in just the right proportions, too. Small, frequent water changes will go a long way toward maintaining balanced, stable water chemistry and taking the guesswork out of trace element supplementation.

Today's reefers rely on synthetic sea salt mixes to formulate their saltwater.

However, even though quality synthetic salt mixes contain all necessary major elements and trace elements for a healthy mini-reef, some critical elements, such as calcium and various buffering compounds, tend to get used up faster than they can be replenished through water changes. This is especially true of mini-reefs that house mostly small-polyped stony corals, which have a high demand for calcium carbonate. Fortunately, the levels of these elements can be tested and supplemented readily and easily via the methods described in the previous chapter.

Testing, Testing!

By now, you've probably gathered that frequent testing of water parameters will be an ongoing and important part of your reef-keeping regimen. At the very least, you should have the following test kits on hand at all times:

- Ammonia

- Nitrite

- Nitrate

• Calcium

• Alkalinity (carbonate hardness)

• pH

Used regularly, these kits will allow you to keep a good eye on the more important water parameters so you can promptly detect and remedy any adverse trends before they reach crisis proportions.

The Color of Success

Most test kits available to reef keepers are colorimetric. That is, they involve mixing a liquid or dry reagent chemical with a small sample of aquarium water, waiting for the recommended period of time to allow the sample to change color, and then comparing the color of the sample against a color comparator test strip. A sample that is darker in color will have a higher concentration of the element you are testing for, and vice versa.

Mushrooms are fairly basic in their water requirements.

In some cases, though, colorimetric tests can get quite elaborate, involving the addition of chemicals in multiple stages (sometimes including both liquid and powder) and then adding a liquid chemical drop by drop until the water sample turns a certain color. In these cases, the number of drops required to bring about the color change will indicate the concentration of the element you are testing for.

Ammonia, nitrite, nitrate, and pH test kits often fall into the former category, while calcium and alkalinity test kits are often of the latter style.

Colorimetric test kits are moderately easy to use and relatively inexpensive. However, it's important to be aware that colorimetric test kits are not all created equal. Some brands have a reputation for producing very accurate results, while others are rather unpredictable.

Regardless of the brand you choose, be sure to keep track of the expiration date of each test kit, and be prepared to discard and replace each kit after this date has passed–even if that means throwing out what would seem to be a perfectly good product. You see, colorimetric test kits truly begin to lose efficacy after their "use by" dates and will, therefore, produce invalid readings. The small amount of money you might save by holding on to expired test kits is hardly worth the harm you might inflict on your livestock in the event that a gradually accumulating pollutant or a potentially lethal imbalance goes undetected.

Another drawback to colorimetric tests is that they can present something of a challenge to those who have difficulty discerning between subtle shades of color. So, if you can't see a difference between "sea foam" and "sea mist" on those color sample cards you get at the paint store, you might need to get a second opinion on your test results. I happen to be one of those people and hence, must always ask my wife to double-check my results. Invariably, my visual perception is off by one color shade–or so she tells me.

Probing Parameters

Several water parameters, such as pH, salinity, temperature, dissolved oxygen, and redox potential, can be monitored using digital electronic meters with submersible probes. If properly calibrated and maintained, the better units give accurate and reliable readings. They're also convenient to use and don't require the aquarist to trifle with caustic liquid chemicals or fumble with those tiny foil pouches that powder reagents are typically packaged in.

On the downside, you get what you pay for with electronic probes. The cheap ones provide the least accurate readings–and adding insult to injury, they are significantly more costly than even the most accurate colorimetric test kit. Conversely, the most accurate electronic meters are also the most expensive, making them impractical choices for the average penny-pinching reefer.

The Flamingo Tongue is a rare little beauty that does very well in aquariums with excellent water chemistry.

Water Movement Makes a Healthy Mini-Reef

No book about mini-reef aquariums would be complete without a discussion of water movement. The waters around natural coral reefs are in constant motion due to ever-changing tides, fickle currents, and rolling waves. Not surprisingly, the eddying, swirling, and surging action of water is vital to the health of corals and other sessile invertebrates that call the reef home.

Out With the Bad Water, In With the Good

Vigorous water movement also assists in exporting coral waste products and facilitates the sloughing of mucous or organic film that is so vital to the health of certain invertebrates. For example, leather corals (a large group of soft corals so

Stony corals need good water circulation to keep sediment and wastes from accumulating on them.

named because of the rough, leathery feel of their tissue when their polyps are retracted) routinely close up and develop a waxy-looking film that sheds a few days later, ridding the coral of settled debris or algae growing on its surface. Without vigorous water movement, leather corals in the mini-reef are unable to shed this waxy layer properly and may remain closed up for prolonged periods. The aquarist may then suspect that water parameters are out of balance when the only problem is inadequate water movement.

Keep 'em In Suspense

A mini-reef with ample water movement tends to be a cleaner mini-reef. Why? Constantly moving water keeps debris suspended in the water column rather than allowing it to settle onto the rocks or substrate. While in suspension, debris can be more readily trapped by prefilter media as the water continually circulates through the system. The aquarist can then rinse the prefilter media, eliminating the debris from the mini-reef before it decomposes and degrades water quality.

Fast Food Delivery

Sessile reef invertebrates, by their very nature, are unable to detach themselves from the substrate and chase down prey items. So, if you can't bring the invertebrates to the food, you have to bring the food to the invertebrates, so to speak. That's where water movement comes in.

While it's true that "photosynthetic" invertebrates derive much of their nutrition from the symbiotic zooxanthellae residing in their tissues, many benefit from–or some would say, require–supplemental feedings of plankton. Without vigorous water movement, the waiting tentacles and miniscule mouths of coral polyps and other reef invertebrates would be deprived of the myriad planktonic organisms that drift through the water column.

Well, the same holds true for the mini-reef. A healthy, thriving reef aquarium will produce a plethora of tiny planktonic larvae and other organisms that are a

The rings of small arms around the outside edge of these zoanthids are their feeding tentacles.

welcome addition to the diet of many invertebrates. And even though these invertebrates reside in a closed system, they still depend largely on water movement to deliver the goods.

Spawning Assistance

On the natural coral reefs, water movement plays a major role in the synchronized coral spawning events that occur on a massive scale–often over vast tracts of reef–at around the same time each year.

For example, in the Florida Keys, various corals, including certain *Montastraea* and *Acropora* species, spawn just after sunset a few days after the full moon in August (or somewhere thereabouts), releasing tiny gamete bundles into the water column, which rupture at the surface, releasing eggs and sperm. The corals do not self fertilize, however, so the eggs and sperm from one coral head must encounter the eggs and sperm from a separate coral head for fertilization to occur. Shortly after the eggs are fertilized, they develop into larvae, which are carried with the currents until they (hopefully) settle on a suitable substrate and begin new coral colonies that in turn grow into new coral reefs. Similar synchronous events occur on a much larger scale, and involving a much greater diversity of species, on Australia's Great Barrier Reef, the Flower Garden Banks National Marine Sanctuary in the Gulf of Mexico, and in other locations.

As you can tell from this rudimentary description of the Keys spawning event, water movement is of the utmost importance in the sexual reproduction and distribution of coral species.

Go With the Turbulent Flow

Given all the influences that produce water movement on the coral reef, it stands to reason that the invertebrates are exposed to almost continuous turbulent water flow–random flow coming from several different directions at once–rather than laminar flow, which is linear and comes from only one direction.

Creating turbulent flow in the mini-reef is challenging but achievable. Turbulence can be produced by strategically placing and directing powerheads so that their effluents intersect, are diffused through rockwork, or are deflected off the aquarium glass. The water return nozzle from your sump–or other external devices that deliver effluent with moderate force–can also be directed in a strategic manner to help create turbulence.

Part 3

Never aim a powerhead or return nozzle directly at a coral specimen or other invertebrate, because this will, at best, irritate the specimen, or at worst, cause serious damage or death. For instance, directing a powerhead toward a large-polyped stony coral, such as a bubble coral, for a prolonged period might actually cause its tissue to detach from the skeleton, which would, in all likelihood, prove fatal to the animal.

Making Waves (and Surge)

Today, reef aquarists have an advantage over our reef-keeping forebears in that there are numerous commercially manufactured products available for providing random water movement apart from the standard powerhead.

For instance, you can buy oscillating powerheads, which direct their flow in a sweeping fashion, much the same way an oscillating lawn sprinkler does. Or you can purchase an electronic wavemaker, which is an external unit that allows you to program multiple powerheads to turn on and off in an alternating pattern, producing a simulated wave effect in the aquarium. Another form of wavemaker is the wave timer, which essentially looks like an electrical outlet strip. However, it differs in that the outlets can be adjusted to manipulate the frequency of the waves produced. There are even non-electric wavemakers that you can plumb in line with your return pump. These units automatically produce alternating flow from two separate outputs in response to water pressure.

Surge makers, which typically are do-it-yourself projects, produce water turbulence in a manner very different from wavemakers, wave timers, or oscillating powerheads. The purpose of a surge maker is to cause a large volume of water to suddenly rush into the mini-reef system, replicating the dynamic effect of ocean waves crashing on a shallow reef.

Without getting too heavily into the details, a popular surge system works like this: Water is pumped from the mini-reef up to a surge tank located above the display tank. A PVC siphon pipe extends from inside the surge tank down to the display tank. As water fills the surge tank, the siphon pipe begins to fill simultaneously. Once the surge tank is completely full, the water is sucked down the siphon pipe and into the display tank faster than the pump can refill the surge tank. The siphoning action is broken after all the water flows out and the siphon pipe starts to suck air. Then the surge tank begins to fill with water again, and the whole process repeats itself.

Part 3

Eric Borneman, in his book *Aquarium Corals: Selection, Husbandry and Natural History* (T.F.H. Publications, 2001), describes a do-it-yourself surge device, which uses components found in your toilet tank. I would recommend that you add his book to your research library, not only for a thorough description of his device, but also because it provides a wealth of other reef-keeping information.

Avoiding Dead Spots

However you choose to provide water movement in your mini-reef, be on the lookout for "dead spots," or areas in the tank that are somehow missed by water flow. You can usually identify dead spots by the excessive buildup of detritus that is typical of these areas. Since there's no water movement in dead spots to keep the detritus suspended, the live rock in these areas soon becomes coated with a thick layer of gunk. Not only is this layer detrimental to the organisms encrusting the rock and the process of denitrification that should be taking place within the rock, but it also serves as a perfect "potting soil" for hair algae to become established in.

Areas of low water flow also promote the development of cyanobacteria–so-called slime algae or blue-green algae (ironically, it is neither blue-green nor a form of algae)–which forms loose, slimy sheets on the rocks and substrate. By simply increasing water flow to areas repeatedly affected with cyanobacteria, many aquarists have been able to eliminate this problem once and for all.

Different Corals Need Different Water Movement

So, we've established that energetic, turbulent water flow is desirable in a mini-reef and that dead spots are to be discouraged. The water-movement picture is a bit more complicated than that on natural coral reefs, however. The different zones of the coral reef are subject to water movement of varying intensity and characteristics. On the coral reef, you'll find shallow areas that are continually buffeted with powerful surge, deeper areas where water

Flowerpot corals do best with moderate water movement coming from multiple directions.

movement is relatively moderate, and everything in between. In each area of the reef, corals and other invertebrates can be found that are perfectly adapted to the local conditions.

So, taking all that into consideration, we don't necessarily need to deliver equally vigorous water movement to every area in a mini-reef, right? For instance, many small-polyped stony corals (*Acropora* spp., *Montipora* spp., and *Porites* spp., etc.) prefer highly energetic water movement, while many large-polyped stony corals (*Trachyphyllia* spp., *Plerogyra* spp., and *Catalaphyllia* spp., etc.) prefer gentle to moderate water movement. Soft corals also vary considerably in their water-movement preferences.

As you've undoubtedly deduced already, the differing water-movement requirements of sessile invertebrates must be taken into consideration when determining where to place them in the mini-reef. With some finicky specimens, the aquarist may need to redirect powerheads or experiment with placement a little, moving the animal to different locations until an area with the appropriate amount and quality of water movement is found.

Part Four

"well, that's odd. The guy at the pet store said animals love those things"

Stocking Up

Congratulations! You've finally reached the point where your patience begins to pay off. You've completed the somewhat laborious setup phase, and now it's time to have some fun! It's time to start purchasing livestock for your new mini-reef.

But where to begin? How do you go about choosing a healthy and compatible assortment of corals and other reef invertebrates that will transform your newly set up mini-reef into the thriving microcosm you've been dreaming of?

Start with a Reputable Dealer
Step one on the road to successful stocking is finding a reputable reef aquarium dealer. This

The time has come to begin adding corals to your mini-reef.

person will likely be a local small-business owner with whom you can develop an ongoing relationship based on trust. The right dealer is someone who instills confidence in you through his expertise and through the quality of his livestock, who takes the time to develop an understanding of your aquarium setup, and who treats you like a valued customer rather than a pocketbook waiting to be emptied.

If necessary, do a little shopping around for a dealer who satisfies these criteria—even if it means driving a few extra miles. Don't just settle on the closest dealer, assuming they're all cut from the same cloth. They're not. Besides, an unqualified or unscrupulous dealer can cost you a lot of extra cash and cause you a lot of unnecessary headaches further down the road.

Be sure to look over a prospective dealer's tanks to determine how diligently he maintains them. Do they look neglected? Choked with hair algae? Overrun with *Aiptasia*? Are dead or dying specimens present in the tanks? If so, do an abrupt about face and head for another shop. You may not be able to judge a book by its cover, but you can certainly judge an aquarium dealer by the content of his or her aquariums!

Many corals are displayed on holders in pet shops.

Buying Livestock Online

More and more reef keepers are turning to the Internet to purchase corals and other marine livestock. The advantage of buying livestock online is that, with so many Internet sources out there vying for customers, you usually have a greater selection to choose from than you'll see in most local aquarium shops. Also, buying livestock through the Internet can be a bit less expensive than buying locally. However, keep in mind that shipping charges can, in some cases, negate any savings you might enjoy when buying online.

On the downside, buying livestock online amounts to an act of faith. There's no way to look over specimens for evidence of health problems or just to be sure you're getting the mature specimen you ordered rather than a smaller, less valuable fragment. What you get is what they send you.

Chapter 15

Each specimen should also be examined for evidence of disease or ill health. Look for:

- Dark discoloration, sunken lesions, or holes.
- Tissue that is obviously receding or detaching from the skeleton.
- Jelly-like matter clinging to the specimen.
- Gaping mouth(s).
- Contraction that cannot be attributed to normal factors (still acclimating to the dealer's tank, lights just coming on, routine shedding of leather corals, etc.).
- Other specimens in the same tank that appear unhealthy or on the verge of death (your specimen might not be far behind!).

Evidence of physical damage due to careless collection or handling practices—torn tissue, crudely broken "branches," etc.—should also give you cause for concern about a specimen. While many corals will respond remarkably well to such mechanical assaults under otherwise normal conditions, the added stress of shipping and repeated reacclimation can leave mechanically damaged invertebrates highly susceptible to secondary infections that often do them in. It's best to leave any damaged specimen in your dealer's tank. Don't try to convince yourself that you'll be able to nurse it back to health, because chances are you won't succeed. Also, you don't want to "reward" improper collection and handling techniques by purchasing a specimen that has been damaged in this fashion.

Also, you've got potential logistical problems associated with shipping to consider. For instance, what is your insurance against lost specimens due to improper handling in transit? What happens if the package gets misdirected, it arrives days late at your home, and all the corals are either dead or stressed to the point that survival is unlikely? How do you get compensation for lost livestock? It's a good idea to ask these questions ahead of time so you know exactly who is liable in the event of a shipping catastrophe.

Before buying livestock online, I would strongly urge you (once again) to visit some Internet reef-keeping forums to get opinions and testimonials about various online sources from other forum members. Believe me, reef keepers are more than willing to share their online-shopping triumphs and tragedies.

Choosing Healthy Livestock

If you're buying from a local source and therefore have the luxury of examining potential purchases for signs of ill health, by all means, give each specimen a thorough visual

Part 4

examination before buying. You don't have to be an expert on sessile invertebrate health to identify some telltale warning signs.

First, look at the color of the specimen. Does it look unnaturally pale and faded? If so, the specimen might be "bleached," which means it has "dumped" its symbiotic zooxanthellae as a result of excessive stress and will not likely survive in your aquarium. If you're not sure what the natural color of the specimen should be, then you should spend a little time with a good coral ID book before buying.

Prior knowledge of natural appearance is important because not all coral specimens are supposed to be brightly or richly colored. For instance, many soft corals, such as the leather corals, colt corals, and *Xenia* corals, are rather subdued in coloration, ranging from off-white to taupe to subtly pinkish. The large, fleshy polyps of some LPS corals, especially the bubble corals and elegance corals, are also naturally whitish in color.

So What's in a Common Name?

A significant challenge that reef keepers often face is knowing exactly what species of invertebrate they're actually buying–the reason being, most dealers simply don't identify their invertebrate livestock to the species level. At best, they might identify the genus, but more often than not, a common name is all that is given. This is understandable, since differentiating between similar coral species within a given genus is difficult even for the experts. To further complicate matters, corals of the same species can have radically different growth habits, depending on which zone of the reef they were collected from. For instance, certain *Acropora* species may have a compact, bushy growth habit, a table-like growth habit, a branching growth habit, or a variety of other forms depending on the amount and quality of water movement they are subjected to.

If corals are so hard to identify to the species level, what's the big deal about identifying them by common name? Well, as with identifying any group of animals or plants, common names can lead to confusion when the same (or very similar) common name is used to describe more than one coral species. Take the name tree coral, for example. This common name is applied to numerous similarly shaped soft coral species belonging to several different genera, some of which are well suited to aquarium life, while others are nearly impossible to keep alive. Or how about the name brain coral? This moniker is applied to several boulder-like small-polyped stony corals as well as to several species of large-polyped stony coral.

The bottom line is that common names don't provide much useful information about a given specimen–certainly not enough to help the aquarist determine appropriate care. The best possible solution to this dilemma is to educate yourself (to the extent possible) about the characteristics and requirements of the commonly sold invertebrate genera before it's time to buy. Never purchase a specimen for which you don't know the proper care requirements–no matter how irresistibly beautiful it may be! Unfortunately, too many novice reef keepers fall into this trap and end up causing the untimely death of perfectly healthy corals, simply because they haven't taken the time to learn how to provide the appropriate care.

Are You Going Soft or Stony?

One question that every reef keeper should answer for him or herself before buying livestock is, Will the mini-reef feature soft corals, stony corals, or a mixture of both? Actually, this question should be answered before purchasing the lighting system, since the direction you choose can make a big difference in the aquarium's lighting requirements.

For example, a mini-reef that is intensely illuminated with 400-watt metal halide lamps might be suitable for light-hungry small-polyped stony (SPS) corals and *Tridacna* clams, but it would be grossly overilluminated for many popular soft corals and large-polyped stony (LPS) corals. That's not to say that those organisms wouldn't like the light, though. On the other hand, a mini-reef illuminated with lower intensity fluorescent or compact fluorescent lamps, which might be perfect for many softies and LPS corals, would be grossly under illuminated for many SPS corals.

If you want the best of both worlds and decide to go with a mixed tank that includes both soft and stony corals, you'll obviously need to choose a middle-of-the-road lighting configuration that satisfies the needs of both. You'll also need to place your corals in appropriate locations in the tank so that the light-hungry SPS corals are near the crest of your mini-reef (i.e., right under the lights) and the soft corals are in the mid- to lower regions of the tank.

Small-polyped stony corals are usually recommended only after you have had some experience.

Another important consideration when mixing soft and stony corals in the same aquarium is that you may be confronted with compatibility issues. We'll get into the subject of coral compatibility in greater detail in a later chapter, but suffice it to say that certain SPS and soft corals often won't suffer one another's presence lightly!

Now More Than Ever: The Quarantine Tank

Aquarists of all areas of specialization are constantly admonished in aquarium literature and by their fellow aquarists to quarantine new specimens for several weeks before introducing them to the main aquarium. Some are diligent in their quarantine practices; others can't be bothered with quarantining and instead put their trust in the fates to protect their established aquariums from any negative fallout.

Let me assure you that this latter approach is a ticking time bomb when it comes to mini-reef aquariums. The quarantine process is of the utmost importance for new corals and other sessile invertebrates. If you fail to quarantine new specimens, it's only a matter of time before disaster will strike. After spending so much time, money, and energy getting your mini-reef up and running, why take a chance on the health of your mini-reef livestock by failing to quarantine?

A quarantine period is definitely recommended for all animals.

The invertebrate quarantine tank does not need to be large or especially complicated, but it must provide adequate lighting, water movement, and biological filtration, as well as the proper water temperature.

A ten-gallon tank can be outfitted for this purpose easily and inexpensively. Lighting can be provided via small but appropriately rated fluorescent or power compact tubes. A single powerhead should suffice for water movement. A few chunks of quality live rock will provide adequate biological filtration. And a small submersible heater can be used to maintain the correct temperature.

Remember, your quarantine tank only needs to hold a new specimen for a few weeks while you monitor it for signs of ill health or pests (e.g., *Aiptasia*) that might be hiding on it or the rock it's attached to. Once you're satisfied that the specimen is healthy and not a vector for introducing some nasty parasite, you can introduce it to the mini-reef.

Of course, you must also remember to quarantine new fish before introducing them to the mini-reef. While diseases of fish will not likely affect the sessile invertebrates in your system, there are the other fish to consider. A sick fish introduced to the mini-reef will quickly infect the others and may eventually cause the death of all the fish in the system. Besides, if you observe signs of disease or parasitic infestation only after introducing a fish to the display tank, there's not much you can do to remedy the situation. The medications commonly used to cure the maladies of marine fish–especially copper-based medications– cannot be administered to an aquarium housing sessile invertebrates. Also, capturing and removing a sick fish from a mini-reef is next to impossible without tearing the whole system apart.

Part 4

Fairly Failsafe Corals for the New Reefer

So far, our discussion of stocking has covered issues such as selecting a dealer, buying livestock online, the problem with common names, and choosing healthy specimens. But one significant stocking question remains unanswered: Which specific invertebrates are best suited for an aquarist's maiden voyage into mini-reefs?

A Sampling of Soft Corals

Without question, the coral species that are most hardy and tolerant of the beginner's learning curve can be found among the so-called soft corals. Not only are many soft corals rugged and forgiving, but they can also be quite beautiful and interesting in their own right.

Mushrooms are a safe bet for all mini-reefers.

The soft corals are so named because, unlike SPS and LPS corals, they do not produce skeletons of calcium carbonate. Their bodies are, therefore, relatively soft and flexible. They do, however, have tiny spicules of calcium–called sclerites–in their tissues, which lend some support to their flexible bodies. Sclerites are uniquely different from one soft coral species to the next, so comparing these spicules is often the only reliable way for scientists to distinguish between two very similar-looking species.

Learning With Leather Corals

Many a novice reef keeper has gotten his or her figurative feet wet with leather corals. This vast family of corals is composed of a staggering number of genera, only about five of which are well represented in the aquarium trade–*Sarcophyton, Sinularia, Lobophyton, Alcyonium,* and *Cladiella.*

As I mentioned in an earlier chapter, the leather corals get their common name from the fact that their tissues are tough and leathery to the touch when their polyps are retracted. Morphologically speaking, they can be mushroom shaped, tree-like, convoluted, or encrusted with fingerlike lobes. Colors include various shades of brown, beige, white, yellow, green, and even purple.

The polyps of leather corals range from being elongated and prominent, as with the various mushroom leathers (*Sarcophyton* spp.), to being just barely visible, as with many of the finger leathers (*Sinularia* spp.). The polyps retract completely after dark, when the colony is disturbed–such as when a snail or hermit crab crawls over the coral–or in response to any dramatic changes in their living conditions.

Most leather corals adapt extremely well to a variety of aquarium conditions, which is why they are so ideally suited for the beginner's mini-reef. However, in spite of their ruggedness, these corals can be a bit temperamental and may close up for prolonged periods in response to suboptimal water conditions, inappropriate lighting, or inadequate water

Generally speaking, many leather corals are very hardy and make a great beginner coral.

Part 4

movement. The good news is that this problem can usually be remedied quite easily by moving the leather coral to a more suitable location in the mini-reef, by increasing water movement, or by improving the water quality through partial water changes.

As I mentioned earlier, occasional retraction for several days is normal for leather corals and absolutely no cause for alarm. During this shutdown period, the coral will develop a thin waxy coating that will slough off a few days later (with the assistance of water turbulence), revealing a healthy, robust coral specimen.

Other "tree-type" corals, such as Kenyan tree corals, generally also make good beginner corals.

Kenya Tree Coral

Another great choice of soft coral for the novice reefer is the Kenya tree coral (*Capnella imbricata*). Beige to brown in overall color, the Kenya tree coral is certainly not the most flamboyantly colored coral in the sea, but I find subtle beauty in its white-tinged polyps, which look almost as if they have been dipped in icing. If provided with gentle to moderate water movement, the Kenya tree coral's delicate-looking branches will continually drift and sway in a hypnotic fashion.

Like the leather corals, the Kenya tree coral will adapt nicely to a broad range of aquarium conditions. It's also a fast grower that must be allotted a reasonable amount of tank space if it is to reach its full glory. If you start with a small specimen, be sure to consider this coral's growth rate when placing it among other invertebrates.

Don't be surprised if your Kenya tree coral, once it reaches a mature size, begins to drop branches occasionally. This is simply a reproductive strategy that allows the coral to distribute itself over a larger area of reef. In fact, you'll be pleased to discover that the branches that land on a suitable substrate will promptly attach themselves and begin to grow new colonies.

Feel the Pulse!

A personal favorite among the soft corals is the group collectively known as the pulse corals (*Xenia* spp.), or pulsing *Xenia.* As the name implies, the feathery tentacles of each polyp continually pulse opened and closed in a rhythmic fashion. The visual effect is quite mesmerizing–sort of like watching time-lapse photography of flower petals as they open and close. In fact, people viewing my mini-reef for the first time typically lean over, squint their eyes as if they can hardly believe what they're seeing, and ask, "Are they moving by themselves, or is the current doing that?"

When properly cared for, Xenia will spread quite nicely along the live rock in your aquarium.

The colors of these delightful corals can be creamy white, brown, green, or delicate pink, and under proper conditions, they grow and reproduce at a staggering rate, rapidly colonizing adjacent rocks and virtually any surface, including the glass panes of the aquarium. The individual colonies, which typically arise from a single stalk, are capable of detaching themselves and moving with surprising speed (as corals go) toward areas with more favorable conditions. Whenever pulse corals move, they invariably leave behind small clumps of tissue, which soon give rise to new colonies. This is a perfect and readily observable example of the asexual reproductive strategy known as pedal laceration.

I should point out that not all *Xenia* species pulse, and even those that do will sometimes inexplicably stop pulsing in the aquarium. This cessation of pulsing has been attributed to improper iodine levels, pH being too low or too high, insufficient lighting, and numerous other factors, but all of these explanations are purely anecdotal or speculative. Scientific research has yet to reveal the true cause.

Encrusting *Briareum*

If you're looking for a trulyfoolproof beginner coral, you'll find it among the encrusting *Briareum* species. These corals consist of a flat, smooth mat of tissue, from which emerge numerous closely spaced polyps–looking rather like hairy mats as they envelop every surface or substrate in close proximity. When the polyps are fully retracted, all that is visible is a very thin layer of tissue that conforms to the shape of the substrate.

Briareum species are actually forms of gorgonian. However, they lack the rigid central axis that makes possible the gorgonian's upright, branched growth habit.

The rate of growth is remarkably rapid with these corals. Several years back, I received a single small cutting of *Briareum*, consisting of, at the most, five polyps. Since then, that tiny colony has expanded to hundreds of polyps, encrusting multiple rocks in my tank, which now have taken on the appearance of a beautiful grassy hill. I've even traded several *Briareum*-encrusted rocks with a couple of the dealers in my area for new livestock or merchandise.

Similar to Briareum, Green Star Polyps grow at a remarkable rate if conditions are optimum.

As you've probably deduced, the only problem you might encounter with growing *Briareum* is its tendency to take over too much valuable reef real estate and that you'll need to thin some of it out on occasion to keep it under control.

Get Shroomin'!

Our next group of beginner-friendly invertebrates is the mushroom corals, mushroom anemones, or corallimorphs (belonging to the order Corallimorpharia). Mushroom corals come by their name honestly, each polyp having a flat, rounded growth habit reminiscent of the terrestrial fungi. But that's where the similarity ends.

Each "mushroom" is actually an individual polyp with a clearly visible mouth located in the center of the disk. Most mushrooms lack the defined tentacles of true corals, but some exhibit greatly reduced tentacles in the form of bumps, warts, or tiny hair-like appendages (as with the "hairy mushrooms").

The show-stopping colors of 'shrooms must be seen to be believed–various shades and combinations of green, blue, red, purple, orange, and just about every other color imaginable. Some are solid colored. Some sport polka dots. Some are variegated, mottled, or marbled.

Mushrooms come in many colors and textures, from green to red and smooth to pimply.

When conditions are right, mushrooms will frequently reproduce themselves by dividing across the oral disk. You can often tell that division is imminent when two opposing points on the margin of the oral disk begin to draw inward. Soon thereafter, a second mouth is formed, and the animal divides into two distinct individuals. The process is quite fascinating to observe.

There is one caveat to keep in mind with mushroom corals: While they are extremely forgiving of the occasional water-quality misstep by the novice reef keeper, they cannot tolerate intense lighting, such as that produced by metal halide lamps. A lower position in a moderately lit mini-reef will serve these animals well, and they'll reward you by producing lots of offspring that you can spread around the tank or trade with your dealer or fellow reef keepers. If you simply must keep mushrooms in a brightly lit tank, place them at the bottom, preferably beneath an overhanging rock where they won't be exposed to the full intensity of the lamps.

Meet the Zoanthids!

No beginner's mini-reef is complete without at least a few species of zoanthid polyp. The zoanthids, also called button polyps, sea mats, or colonial anemones, are among the easiest coral reef invertebrates to maintain in captivity. If there's a way to bring about the demise of these polyps apart from intentionally pouring poison into the water, I'm not aware of it. Okay, so I'm exaggerating–but not by much!

The zoanthids' iron constitution stems from the conditions under which many species prosper in nature. While zoanthids occur at varying depths and on various zones on the coral reef, many commonly sold varieties are found in shallow, turbulent areas, which may be left high and dry at low tide. Hence, zoanthids can adapt remarkably well to a broad range of aquarium conditions. However, when lighting intensity is grossly inadequate, zoanthids may elongate their stalks in an unnatural fashion as if trying to stretch their oral disks up toward the light.

A Note of Caution About Zoanthid Polyps

While easy to propagate in the mini-reef and beautiful to behold, zoanthids produce a potent neuro-toxin, called palytoxin, that can make humans extremely ill or even cause death. In fact, some Pacific Islanders have been known to tip their spears and arrows with this toxin to bring down their quarry quickly. The toxin is produced both within the polyp and in the slimy mucus that coats the animal. Accidental poisoning sometimes occurs after an unwary aquarist handles zoanthids and later, absentmindedly, puts his fingers in or near his mouth and ingests some of the toxin. Poisoning can also occur through breaks in the skin—usually when handling zoanthids with bare hands. As a routine precaution, always wear rubber gloves when handling zoanthids. If you don't wear gloves, it's imperative to wash your hands promptly afterward.

Zoanthid species all follow the same basic morphology—a button-shaped oral disk with a mouth in the center atop a short, stubby stalk. The margin of the oral disk is ringed with tentacles, the length of which varies from species to species. Most zoanthids, such as the popular *Zoanthus sociatus*, are under an inch in diameter, but some can get larger. The stunningly beautiful *Protopalythoa grandis* can exceed two inches in diameter. Zoanthid colonies may consist of individual, unconnected polyps, or the polyps may arise from a shared layer of encrusting tissue called a stolon, or coenenchyme.

Zoanthids are some of the easiest corals out there to care for.

Zoanthid colors are quite diverse, including shades of green, brown, gray, blue, yellow, and orange. Many species exhibit multiple colors on a single polyp. For instance, you might see a zoanthid polyp that has a bright orange center surrounded by white with dark green tentacles—or any number of color combinations.

The LPS Short List

More and more reef keepers are falling in love with the large-polyped stony (LPS) corals these days—not only for their unsurpassed splendor, but also for their fascinating behavior and relative ease of maintenance.

Part 4

LPS corals are large, single, fleshy polyps that emerge from calcareous cone- or bowl-shaped skeletons. At first glance, one might wonder whether LPS corals have a skeleton at all, as it is typically obscured completely by the animal's tissues. However, at night, when the polyp retracts, the skeleton is more plainly visible.

Most of the commonly sold LPS corals come from shallow lagoons or seagrass beds, where they sit directly on the substrate with their skeletons often buried in the sand or silt. You usually will not find these animals on the reef proper (though there are exceptions) and consequently, they do not belong nestled up in the rockwork of your mini-reef, either. When placed too high in the mini-reef, these top-heavy corals have a tendency to tumble down due to the workings of motile invertebrates or careless aquarists who accidentally bump them when rearranging rockwork or performing routine aquarium maintenance. As a result, the coral's delicate tissue may become damaged, which then could lead to secondary infection and, ultimately, the death of the animal.

Do these beautiful corals a favor and place them on the substrate, their skeletons partially buried as they would be in nature. They really are ideal stand-alone specimens that deserve a prominent position toward the front of the mini-reef, anyway!

Open brain corals usually do well in mini-reefs that have excellent lighting and water quality.

Keep An Open Brain

When I first laid eyes on the fluorescent-green and chocolate-brown open brain coral (*Trachyphyllia geoffroyi*) that now resides in my mini-reef, I knew I had to have it–and I also knew I had the ideal location for it in my tank. The only problem was, another customer at my dealer's shop was eyeing the specimen, too, and he was in line ahead of me!

Imagine my "dismay" when I heard my dealer explain to the customer–who had a fish-only aquarium–that his lighting was not sufficient to sustain the coral! "Oh, that's a shame," I gushed sympathetically as the poor chap walked toward the door, crestfallen. Before the bell on the screen door even stopped jingling, I plopped my credit card down on the counter and proclaimed triumphantly, "I'll take it!"

Part 4

Why such enthusiasm for this species? Well, for one thing, the colors of open brain corals are unparalleled among many common reef invertebrates–with the possible exception of the *Tridacna* clams and certain *Acropora* species. Specimens can sport fluorescent shades of green, pink, purple, and red, or various combinations thereof. Under actinic lighting, their colors become absolutely surreal!

This coral's convoluted tissue gives rise to its common name, looking, as it does, like an exposed brain–a gruesome bit of imagery for such an attractive coral! The animal can inflate or deflate these meandering tissues in response to changing light levels. In lower light, the tissues inflate fully to allow the maximum amount of light to reach the symbiotic zooxanthellae. Conversely, the tissues deflate proportionately in response to intense lighting. Open brain corals also inflate in order to rid themselves of sand or detritus that accumulates on their tissues.

The open brain corals' short feeding tentacles, which line the lobes of their tissues, are generally withdrawn during the day unless they detect food in the water. However, at night, the polyps emerge to trap whatever plankton happens to settle on the coral. It's notable that these animals are completely non-aggressive toward tank mates and lack the potent stinging tentacles typical of some LPS species.

From Brains to Bubbles

Another LPS coral that's perfectly at home in the beginner's mini-reef is the bubble coral (*Plerogyra sinuosa*). The tentacles of this delightful coral are modified into round or elliptical bubbles, which greatly increase the amount of tissue surface area– and hence, the amount of symbiotic zooxanthellae– exposed to sunlight. This adaptation serves bubble corals well in nature, where they usually occur in low-light areas. Ironically, though, they adapt quite readily to brighter lighting schemes in the aquarium, provided they are given a reasonable period to adjust.

Bubble corals are popular with reefers, but beware of their aggressive sweeper tentacles!

Part 4

Bubble corals range in color from pearly white to fawn colored to green and are quite fast growing. When I purchased my specimen, it was approximately four inches in diameter, with its bubbles fully inflated. About one year later, it had easily doubled in size!

As with many LPS corals, bubble corals possess long, stinging "sweeper" tentacles that emerge at night, when the bubbles have deflated. These tentacles are used to sting neighboring invertebrates to keep them from encroaching on the bubble coral's territory. This propensity must be taken into consideration when placing these animals in the mini-reef. Be sure to allow a minimum of six inches around the entire specimen (with its bubbles fully expanded) and any adjacent sessile invertebrates.

The Elegant Elegance Coral

At first glance, it's easy to mistake the elegance coral (*Catalaphyllia jardinei*) for a massive sea anemone with spectacularly graceful tentacles tipped with fluorescent green, pink, purple, orange, or blue. However, when the coral retracts at night, the characteristic conical skeleton is more visible, making it obvious that this animal is, indeed, an LPS coral.

Healthy elegance corals are sometimes mistaken for large anemones.

The magnificently beautiful elegance coral is somewhat more sensitive to fluctuations in water chemistry, lighting, and water movement than some beginner LPS species; however, it is sufficiently hardy for the novice who demonstrates a conscientious approach to reef keeping–which is, after all, what we should be striving for, right?

The elegance coral's only drawback is that it possesses very long stinging tentacles that will seriously damage or kill any invertebrate that comes too close. And since the elegance coral can become quite enormous, it is best kept in a large mini-reef with ample bottom area where it can lay claim to its own spacious patch of substrate. Placed too close to the rockwork, the elegance coral, when fully expanded, might abrade its tissues against the rough edges of the rock, causing injury.

Part 4

And The LPS List Goes On!

Of course, this is just a sample of LPS corals that are suitable for the beginner's mini-reef. You might also want to try your hand at keeping some of these listed below:

• Hammer coral (*Euphyllia ancora*)

• Frogspawn coral (*Euphyllia divisa*)

• Torch coral (*Euphyllia glabrescens*)

• Plate coral (*Heliofungia actiniformis*)

• Trumpet coral (*Caulastrea furcata*)

Step Up to SPS Corals

The SPS corals, or small-polyped stony corals, are the true architects of the reef. Their calcareous skeletons, laid down layer upon layer for thousands of years, are the building blocks that comprise the coral reef structure. In fact, SPS coral polyps are responsible for building the only animal-made structure that is visible from space—Australia's Great Barrier Reef.

I really can't make the claim that there is such thing as a true "beginner" SPS coral. However, after you've taken a little time to master proper reef-keeping techniques with more forgiving specimens first, there's no reason you can't make the jump to SPS corals. But patience is a virtue here. Most SPS species simply cannot endure common beginner errors such as allowing fluctuations in water parameters or providing inadequate lighting or insufficient water movement.

Montipora coral is best left to those hobbyists with some experience under their belts.

Mighty, morphing SPS

When you're finally ready to step up to SPS, you'll no doubt be amazed at the diversity of their

Part 4

morphology. From bushy to boulder-shaped, from tabular to towering, from flat to fingerlike, you'll find just about any shape you can imagine among the SPS corals. Perhaps the greatest diversity of form is found among the myriad species of *Acropora*. These corals represent all of the morphologies listed above and more. For example, the branches of *Acropora formosa* loosely resemble deer antlers–hence the common name staghorn coral. *A. digitifera* has compact, fingerlike branches. And *A. cytherea* grows in the shape of a broad, flat table. Often, wildly different forms can occur within the same species! How is this possible?

For the sake of illustration, take two individual specimens of an *Acropora* species–one occupying a niche on the reef crest where it is constantly pummeled by surge, and another residing in a deep, protected inshore region. Though the two individual specimens belong to the same species, they may take on a radically different appearance over time in response to the prevailing conditions in their respective niches. In this case, the specimen from the reef crest would likely develop very sturdy branches that grow in a relatively compact cluster in response to the constant wave action, while the specimen from the protected inshore region might develop thinner, spindlier branches that are more loosely arranged.

Sounds like a taxonomist's nightmare, doesn't it? Well, that is precisely the reason it is so difficult–even for the experts–to distinguish among the various *Acropora* species (as well as the species of many other SPS genera, for that matter) with any amount of certainty.

A similar taxonomic conundrum exists with the numerous *Montipora* species, which also adapt their forms based on environmental factors, especially water movement. Most reefers envision the broad, flat plating varieties when they think of the genus *Montipora*. However, like the *Acropora* species, *Montipora* corals exhibit considerable plasticity of form, including fingerlike, encrusting, branching, and tabular, depending on where the individual specimen occurs on the reef.

SPS Requirements in the Mini-Reef

Several elements must be present for SPS corals to thrive in the mini-reef. The first critical element is a consistent, stable calcium level of 400-450ppm. SPS corals extract a considerable amount of calcium from the water for skeleton building. Therefore, you must never adopt a lackadaisical approach to calcium supplementation if you intend to keep SPS corals. In fact, it's not uncommon for reefers who are successful in keeping these corals in optimum health to employ more than one method of calcium supplementation, such as the use of a calcium reactor in conjunction with kalkwasser top-offs.

Very intense, high-wattage lighting, such as that provided by metal halide lamps, is also a must for keeping SPS corals. Given that many of the SPS species collected for the aquarium trade are taken from sun-drenched shallows, they simply will not reach their full potential in the mini-reef if provided only moderate light levels.

Small frags of Acropora will grow fast if the proper lighting and water requirements are met.

Thirdly, you cannot skimp on water movement with SPS corals. High-energy turbulent flow will help these sensitive animals rid themselves of waste products and prevent detritus from settling on them and promoting smothering algae growth. The type of dynamic water movement described in the earlier section on surge systems is ideal for SPS corals. Short of this, use several powerheads to create turbulence.

Giants Among Clams

The *Tridacna* clams–or the so-called giant clams–are another group of reef invertebrates that are just slightly beyond the scope of the novice reef keeper and are more appropriate for the intermediate to expert reefer. However, their indescribable beauty makes keeping them an accomplishment well worth striving for.

Essentially, when you're able to provide the stable conditions demanded by SPS corals, you're ready for *Tridacna* clams as well. They, too, demand plenty of calcium to build their calcium carbonate shells and require high-intensity lighting to sustain the symbiotic zooxanthellae residing in their colorful and strikingly patterned mantles.

There are a few significant distinctions between the conditions demanded by SPS corals and those of the giant clams. That is, giant clams seem to thrive in aquariums with a small amount of dissolved nutrients in the water, whereas this condition would be detrimental

Tridacna clams commonly have brilliant coloration throughout their mantles.

to the growth and development of SPS corals. Also, these animals prefer gentle to moderate turbulence rather than the high-energy water movement demanded by SPS corals.

Several giant clam species are available to reef hobbyists, and they differ significantly in coloration (even within the same species) and mature size. The breathtaking mantle colors of *Tridacna* clams, which are produced by specialized pigment cells called iridophores, include various shades and combinations of blue, green, purple, and yellow. Mature sizes range from approximately 6 inches for the smallest species, *T. crocea,* to upwards of 48 inches for *T. gigas,* the true "giant clam." In between (and in order of ascending mature size), you've got *T. Maxima, T. squamosa,* and *T. derasa.* Of course, the mature size of these animals must correspond to the size of the aquarium in which they will be housed.

Like most LPS corals, the *Tridacna* clams are typically placed on the floor of the mini-reef so that they can burrow their shells into the substrate. Given the show-stopping coloration of their mantles, which must be positioned so that they face up toward the lights, the substrate is the best location to view giant clams.

Part 4

Acclimation and Invertebrate "Aggression"

Readers with any prior aquarium experience already know how important it is to gradually acclimate fish to new tank conditions. Proper acclimation techniques are even more critical when it comes to introducing invertebrates to the mini-reef, because many corals and other sessile reef invertebrates are highly sensitive to osmotic shock caused by sudden changes in specific gravity.

No matter how closely your aquarium conditions replicate those of the invertebrate's natural habitat, it's still imperative to follow proper acclimation protocol. After all, from the point of collection to the point of arrival at your local aquarium store, the invertebrate was likely

Within the beautiful "anchors" of this anchor coral are dangerous sweeper tentacles.

subjected to extremely varied lighting, temperature, and water quality as it was moved from one holding vessel to another. Therefore, a sudden introduction of this already stressed animal to your aquarium, even if the conditions are close to optimal, might just be the straw that breaks the camel's back.

Proper Acclimation Begins with Proper Handling

The correct acclimation of invertebrates should begin when your dealer is bagging up your specimen so you can take it home. If the animal is handled inappropriately and injured at this time, proper acclimation on your part will do little to save the specimen.

Some corals and other reef invertebrates can tolerate being removed completely from the water and, indeed, survive this experience every day in nature when the tide goes out. However, some should never be removed from the water, because air can get trapped in their tissues and cause necrosis. LPS corals are vulnerable to injury when suddenly exposed to air because, without the support of water, their soft tissues can collapse against their skeletons.

Also, it's imperative to handle invertebrates by either the bases they're attached to, or in the case of LPS corals, by their calcareous skeletons. Never, under any circumstances, grasp invertebrates by their soft tissues.

Space is purposely left between the corals during acclimation.

Don't feel awkward about observing your dealer or his employee closely to make sure your specimen is handled properly, and don't be afraid to refuse the specimen if you think it hasn't been! Most qualified dealers are well versed in proper handling of invertebrates. However, even the best dealers hire inexperienced help from time to time.

Acclimation Protocol

When your specimen is bagged and ready to transport, take it home immediately. Avoid the temptation to run other errands while you're out; make sure that the invertebrate remains in the bag for a minimal amount of time. Once you arrive at home, you should immediately begin the acclimation process.

Part 4

To get started, remove the rubber band and float the bag in your mini-reef so that the temperature in the bag will begin to equalize with the aquarium water. To keep the water in the bag from mixing with your aquarium water right away, drape the top of the bag over the edge of the tank and weigh it down with your light hood or another convenient object.

Then, begin to drip water from your aquarium into the bag at a very slow rate until the water volume in the bag has approximately doubled. At that point, the water parameters in the bag should match those of the aquarium, and the invertebrate can be removed from the bag and placed at the bottom of the mini-reef.

First, lower the bag just slightly below the surface so the animal is not exposed to air. Then grasp the specimen by the skeleton or its base and gently pull it out of the bag, then immediately place it in your mini-reef. Once the specimen has been introduced, remove the bag, water and all, and pour the water down the drain. Avoid dumping water from the bag into your aquarium or you risk introducing any pathogenic organisms that may have come from your dealer's tank.

This phase of the acclimation process should take around 45 minutes to an hour to complete. However, proper acclimation of sessile invertebrates to the intense lighting of the mini-reef aquarium requires a greater investment of time—up to several days in some cases.

Come Into the Light—Slowly

When first introducing invertebrates to your mini-reef, they should be placed at the lowest level of the aquarium–regardless of their lighting requirements in nature. Allow them to remain there until they have completely opened up and appear to be adjusting well to their new environment. Then begin to move them up incrementally to the desired (and species-appropriate) level on the rockwork.

Obviously, species that prefer less intense lighting, such as mushroom polyps, certain soft corals, and LPS corals, don't belong at the highest point in the tank right under the lamps, whereas most light-loving SPS corals will do just fine there.

Keep a close eye on your specimens after each move to ensure that they aren't reacting adversely to the increase in light exposure, and be prepared to move them back down in the event that a negative reaction is noted.

Part 4

You may need to do a little experimentation to determine the ideal level of illumination for some species–and many invertebrates will let you know that they are irritated with their lighting by refusing to expand during daylight hours. Once the right level of illumination has been achieved for a given specimen, it should be left in that location, not moved about randomly to satisfy the whims or aesthetic sensibilities of the aquarist.

Coral Wars: Methods of Self-defense and Domination

Though they may appear benign and inoffensive to the casual observer, many corals and other sessile reef invertebrates are anything but pacifistic and will ruthlessly defend their position on the reef in some surprisingly sinister ways. The reef keeper can readily observe some of these tactics, while others are invisible to the naked eye.

Obnoxious Overgrowth

One of the readily observable forms of coral combat involves the overgrowth of one species by another. This can simply mean that one coral grows more rapidly than its competitor and hence, extends over the smaller coral, depriving it of light. If the overgrown species happens to prefer a low-light environment, this is not necessarily a serious concern. However, if the subordinate coral demands a high level of light, then the shading from the dominant coral might ultimately cause its death. To prevent this, one specimen or the other will have to be moved elsewhere in the tank.

Various types of zoanthid polyps can overgrow valuable reef real estate very quick!.

Overgrowth can also take the form of one coral actually encrusting–i.e., growing directly on–the tissues or skeleton of another. This is a relatively common occurrence when certain fast-growing soft corals, such as *Briareum*, and slow-growing SPS corals are positioned in close proximity to one another. However, it can occur between two soft coral species as well. If the encrusting specimen is left to its own devices, the "encrustee" faces almost certain doom, so the reef keeper must take appropriate precautions (such as providing optimal spacing in the first place and pruning back fast-growing corals) to prevent this form of overgrowth from occurring.

Insidious Stinging

Some sessile invertebrates will nettle the heck out of encroaching neighbors with their tentacles. The feeding tentacles of many invertebrate species are lined with special harpoon-like stinging cells called nematocysts, which can be used to paralyze and capture prey and as a means of attacking competitors and deterring predators. This stinging capacity becomes problematic in the mini-reef only when two coral colonies are placed– or allowed to grow–too close together. Again, it's up to the reef keeper to maintain proper distance between potential competitors so that valued invertebrates aren't needlessly damaged or sacrificed.

In addition to regular feeding tentacles, many LPS and SPS corals develop long "sweeper" tentacles, which can reach surprisingly long distances to sting competitors. Sweeper tentacles typically emerge and do their dirty work at night, so the inexperienced aquarist is often left wondering what is causing the tissue damage on a particular invertebrate when there are no other specimens in close enough proximity to sting it.

Some reef keepers recommend cutting the sweeper tentacles from the offending coral with a razor blade or scalpel so that adjacent specimens aren't continually stung. However, in my humble opinion, injuring a coral–however slightly–to prevent injury to another coral seems a bit barbaric. Besides, it's a temporary solution, as the sweeper tentacles will simply grow back. You and your corals will be much better off if you simply allot adequate space between specimens so that a coral armed with sweeper tentacles can't reach out and touch its neighbors to begin with.

Although easy to care for, horn corals are very capable of delivering a powerful sting.

Invertebrate WMD

If your only experience with aggression in the marine aquarium is that which sometimes manifests itself among coral reef fishes, the last form of coral combat that we'll discuss here (though there are many others) might seem a bit outlandish. It's an invisible form of aggression (except for the results) called allelopathy, which is just a fancy way of saying "coral chemical warfare." You see, many coral species, sponges, and other invertebrates–not to mention various algae–release toxic chemical compounds called terpenoids into the water, which discourage nibbling by predators and parasites and inhibit the encroachment of neighboring organisms.

The biggest offenders when it comes to producing toxic terpenoids are found among the soft corals–especially the leather corals, which are often implicated in the stunted growth, or even death, of their tankmates.

In fact, after introducing a large leather coral specimen to an established mini-reef, it's not uncommon to have other invertebrates in the system suddenly and "mysteriously" retract and refuse to open up. The frustrating thing is, there's no way for the average aquarist to test for the presence of terpenoids. Therefore, the only way to verify that the leather coral is actually the source of the problem–rather than some other water parameter being coincidentally unbalanced–is to remove the newcomer to a quarantine tank temporarily to see whether the problem resolves itself.

On the natural coral reefs, the terpenoids produced by any given specimen have a minimal impact on organisms residing much beyond its immediate vicinity, and the vast ocean waters soon dilute these toxic compounds. In the mini-reef, on the other hand, terpenoids spread rapidly throughout the closed system and can affect all of the invertebrates in the tank. The impact of terpenoids in the mini-reef can be minimized through protein skimming, the regular use of activated carbon, vigorous water movement, and frequent partial water changes.

Part 4

A Myriad of Tiny Mouths

Until fairly recently, it was widely assumed among reef keepers that the so-called photosynthetic corals–those that derive a significant portion of their nutritional needs from the symbiotic zooxanthellae in their tissues–don't require direct feeding on the part of the aquarist in order to thrive in the mini-reef. Indeed, many reefers eschewed feeding their corals altogether to avoid introducing organic matter to the water, which could decompose and degrade water quality.

But with the current shift toward more natural methods of reef keeping, perspectives are beginning to change on the subject of feeding photosynthetic corals. While some still think

Some hobbyists report that flowerpot corals do well if offered food regularly.

feeding is largely unnecessary, others believe corals can never achieve their true growth potential without direct feeding on the part of the aquarist. You might even say that the question of feeding is yet another debate raging among reef keepers today.

So, what's the answer to the feeding question? Well, in my opinion, since science has clearly demonstrated that photosynthetic corals feed actively in nature, we as conscientious reef keepers should also attempt to provide supplemental nutrition for our invertebrate charges beyond the nutrients they receive from symbiotic zooxanthellae.

Coral Feeding Strategies

Okay, so we've established that feeding corals is a good idea, but what exactly can we do with that information? How do we go about providing food items for a group of organisms that vary so considerably in size and morphology? To answer this question, it might be helpful for us to examine some of the strategies that different coral species use to procure their provender.

Some corals feed by snatching or sieving plankton with their tentacles as it drifts past with the current. Others absorb dissolved organic compounds directly from the water through their tissues. Still others engulf and consume relatively large prey items, including small fish. Some even feed by trapping tiny particles and bacteria in a web of mucus, which is drawn into the mouth once the net is full of microscopic munchies. That's just scratching the surface of coral feeding strategies!

By now, you should be getting the picture that there's no one-size-fits-all food item that can be introduced to a mini-reef to satisfy the nutritional needs of all the invertebrate inhabitants. You must tailor your food offerings—especially when it comes to particle size—to the method of prey capture practiced by each coral in your care.

For the sake of illustration, let's compare the feeding strategies of some popular coral varieties, starting with

These large polyps will readily accept small meaty foods.

Part 4

the leather corals. The diminutive tentacles of these soft corals are capable of capturing only the tiniest planktonic particles–much smaller, in fact, than anything we reef keepers can realistically offer. In contrast, the bubble corals, which have relatively enormous mouths, can devour fairly large chunks of seafood, such as shrimp or chopped clam, that are nestled by the aquarist into their bubble-like tentacles. Then there are the open brain corals, which have several small mouths distributed around each polyp. Brine-shrimp-sized particles (preferably vitamin enriched) are just about the perfect sized food for these LPS beauties. Or how about the pulsing *Xenia* corals? They get most of the supplemental nutrition they need through direct absorption, which is the reason pulse corals tend to thrive in water containing at least some dissolved organic compounds but don't seem to do as well in nutrient-poor water.

What Should You Feed?

If your mini-reef is already stocked with corals and other reef invertebrates, then you should already have researched the types of food each of your specimens require. For plankton feeders, numerous commercial invertebrate food preparations are available on the market. These products are very easy to administer and are labeled with specific feeding instructions, which is quite convenient.

A trip to the seafood counter at your local grocer will reveal all kinds of options for corals that prefer to feed upon bits or chunks of seafood, including shrimp, clams, oysters, fresh fish, scallops, and mussels.

I recommend that you purchase small quantities of several different seafood items at once, chop them up into species-appropriate sizes, and then freeze them in small easy-to-feed portions, which can then be thawed out as needed. A small ice cube tray covered with plastic wrap is ideal for apportioning and freezing chopped seafood.

Although baby brine shrimp are commonly fed to corals, they are not nutritionally complete.

If feeding live foods is more up your alley, you might want to experiment with culturing brine shrimp, mysis shrimp, amphipods, or rotifers, depending on the size of prey your corals can consume. A detailed description of the techniques used for culturing these organisms is beyond the scope of this book, but you should be able to find instructions for do-it-yourself culturing projects online.

Target Your Feedings

When feeding corals, it might seem logical to simply drop or pour the food in the water and allow it to drift throughout the aquarium so that it replicates natural plankton, which the corals can feed upon as they would in nature. Indeed, some commercial invertebrate foods are meant to be administered in this fashion. However, there is a significant drawback to this method of feeding. Most of the food will not be captured by corals and instead will settle into the various nooks and crannies throughout the aquarium or end up being trapped in the filter media, where it will begin to decompose. Liquid invertebrate foods administered in this fashion usually end up as foam in the protein skimmer's collection cup.

The preferred method of feeding corals and other reef invertebrates is to shut off all filtration and powerheads so that there is minimal water movement and then target your feedings directly to each specimen. Using a pipette or eyedropper, draw up the food portion and gently release it slightly above the specimen so that it drifts down into its tentacles. Avoid blasting the specimen with a jet of water in the process or it will retract, sensing that it is being attacked, and refuse to feed.

One note of caution about targeted coral feedings with chopped seafood, brine shrimp, or similar food items: If you have planktonivorous fish in your mini-reef, they will soon learn that it's easy to grab these tasty tidbits literally out of the mouths of your corals. Feeding the fish to satiation just prior to feeding the corals can help mitigate this problem, but you may need to gently fend off some of the more voracious piscine specimens while your corals feed.

How Often Should You Feed?

As you'll notice, I haven't yet made any mention of the desired frequency of feeding for sessile invertebrates. Well, there's a good reason for that! There really aren't any fixed rules that govern how frequently invertebrates should be fed in the mini-reef. Sessile invertebrates, by nature, feed only opportunistically. They can't detach themselves and hunt down prey, and they certainly can't depend on plankton drifting their way at regular, predictable intervals–hence they have evolved the symbiotic relationship with "light hungry" zooxanthellae.

Given the fact that we are unable to feed invertebrates according to a timetable preordained by Mother Nature, a little experimentation in both quantity and frequency of feeding becomes necessary. You'll have to maintain a delicate balance between the benefits your invertebrates will receive from direct feeding and the potential negative ramifications associated with excessive or overly frequent feedings. So, the bottom line here is that less is more. Start by offering very small feedings spaced a couple of weeks apart. Then, if all goes well with that regimen, you can experiment with feeding in closer intervals and/or in slightly larger quantities. But again, always err on the side of feeding less, or else you risk overburdening your aquarium's biological filtration capacity as well as promoting blooms of coral-smothering microalgae.

Plankton Smorgasbord: the Refugium

The use of a refugium brings reef keepers about as close as they can get to natural feeding in the closed, artificial system of the mini-reef. What exactly is a refugium? Essentially, it is a tank separate from the display aquarium (some are designed to hang on or in the display aquarium) that shares the same system water but cannot be accessed from the display tank by predatory fish or motile invertebrates. Since predators can't enter, the refugium becomes a safe haven for all kinds of tiny crustaceans, mollusks, worms, echinoderms, and their respective larvae.

A bunch of *Caulerpa* in a refugium.

While predators can't get in, the miniscule invertebrates and their spawn can certainly find their way out of the refugium and into the mini-reef, where they become food for the invertebrates and fish.

Live sand beds and/or pieces of live rock are often installed in refugiums to encourage the proliferation of the desired planktonic organisms. Macroalgae, such as various species of *Halimeda* or *Caulerpa*, might also be cultured in the refugium to assist in the export of dissolved nutrients.

Along with providing an ongoing source of live plankton for mini-reef inhabitants, the protected environment of the refugium is ideal for growing out delicate coral fragments or isolating an injured specimen until it has a chance to heal. In addition, the refugium is quite a fascinating microcosm to observe in and of itself and adds yet another layer of interest to the mini-reef system.

Part 4

Fish in the Mini-Reef

Considering the vast schools and incredible diversity of fish that are found on and around the natural coral reefs, it would seem intuitive that fish are a natural fit in the mini-reef aquarium. However, while I would agree that a mini-reef completely devoid of fish has a sterile and unnatural aspect, I would strongly urge you to restrict your stocking to a small number of reef-friendly specimens.

Remember, the emphasis in the mini-reef should be on the corals and other sessile invertebrates. Anything that detracts from the impeccable water quality they demand is to be avoided. Fish, for all the beauty and interest they provide, can put a heavy burden on water quality with their waste

Clownfishes are probably the most commonly kept species in mini-reef aquariums.

Parrotfishes are NOT good mini-reef aquarium residents unless you no longer wish to keep corals.

Lionfishes need to be fed meaty foods on a regular basis and may become heavy polluters.

products and uneaten food. Besides, fish that are chosen in an indiscriminate fashion can really cause chaos in the mini-reef.

Problem Fish Profiles

What exactly do I mean when I say "reef-friendly fish"? In essence, I'm talking about species that do not fit into any of the following undesirable profiles:

The Polyp Chompers

These fish may be obligate polyp feeders (i.e., they cannot be trained to accept anything else), and include many species of parrotfishes and butterflyfishes. Or they may just nip at the flesh of LPS corals and the mantles of *Tridacna* clams, thereby causing them to remain closed up much of the time. This type of behavior is often observed in many of the large angelfishes of the genus *Pomacanthus,* the dwarf angelfish within the genus *Centropyge,* and some species of tangs and surgeonfishes.

The Heavy Polluters

These can be any large-bodied, predatory species with an appetite to match. The heavy polluter may be completely inoffensive to sessile invertebrates but is prohibited due to its messy eating habits and relatively voluminous waste output. Most of the groupers fall in this category, as do lionfishes and the larger moray eels. In addition, any fish that is regularly overfed will become a heavy polluter as well–yet another good reason to feed sparingly!

The Bull In The China Shop

These fish pose the risk of toppling unstable rockwork and corals through their rambunctious swimming or tunneling

Part 4

behavior. Many of the aforementioned "heavy polluters," especially the moray eels, fit in this category, as do fishes that require more swimming room than the average reef tank allows, including some of the tangs and surgeonfishes.

The Poisonous Pisces

These fish can wipe out an entire mini-reef–invertebrates and fish included–by exuding a toxic slime into the water when stressed. Fortunately, you won't encounter too many fish from this category for sale, but many species of boxfishes and cowfishes exhibit this propensity and, hence, should never be included in the mini-reef. Not to mention, they would be nibbling on the reef anyway.

The Pugilist

Any fish that continually detracts from the serenity of the mini-reef due to its pugnacious approach to other fish belongs in this category. Most triggerfish species can be considered pugilists, not only because they tend to "sample" other fish with their powerful jaws, but also because they may turn their attention–and their impressive dentition–toward sessile invertebrates.

Ironically, some fish that are capable of being quite territorial toward conspecifics (members of their same species) and other species of similar size or coloration are perfectly suited for life in the mini-reef. These potential pugilists include the dottybacks, damsels, and clownfishes. As long as you consider this proclivity, however, these potential pugilists should pose no problem in the mini-reef.

Groupers, even small ones, will usually make short work of expensive shrimps and other inverts.

To help minimize territorial aggression from these otherwise reef-friendly fish, it's recommended that you stock them one to a tank and introduce the potential pugilist last (or at the same time as the other fish). That way, the more aggressive fish will not have the opportunity to claim the whole aquarium as its territory before the other fish arrive.

Part 4

The Trouble with Removing Troublemakers

Why worry ahead of time about fish becoming problematic in the mini-reef? Why not just buy the ones that appeal to you aesthetically, and if one should become a problem for some reason later on, just return it to your dealer? Unfortunately, it's seldom that simple. Once a fish has been introduced to a mini-reef, with its abundance of hiding places and escape routes, capturing and removing it often proves very difficult without tearing apart the entire system, and such an event may cause excessive stress to your invertebrates.

This also applies to catching and removing sick fish from a mini-reef system. Ailing fish can be surprisingly agile and challenging to catch once they see the net coming and fear they are being attacked, which is yet another argument for quarantining all specimens before introducing them to the mini-reef.

The Roster of Reef-Friendly Fishes

Okay, now that we've explored the profiles of fishes that we don't want in the mini-reef, let's take a look at some of the fishes that we do want to include. The following list is by no means exhaustive, but it will certainly give you a good starting point. Each of the species mentioned is relatively easy for beginners to feed and care for, commonly sold, and usually available for a reasonable price.

The yellow-striped maroon clownfish is a popular species among reefers.

The Clownfishes

The fish that first won me over to marine aquarium keeping was the common clownfish (*Amphiprion ocellaris*). There's just something about the comically clumsy swimming motion and the stunning orange and white coloration of this fish (which looks almost painted on) that make it irresistible. Many other clownfish species within the *Amphiprion* genus (and one belonging to a separate genus, *Premnas*) are equally attractive and suitable for the mini-reef.

The well-known symbiosis between the various clownfish species and Pacific anemones–not to mention depictions in popular movies, such as Disney/Pixar's *Finding Nemo*–has made these fish, for many, emblems of the coral reef.

Part 4

While we're on the subject of the famous clownfish/anemone symbiosis, it is not recommended that novice aquarists attempt to recreate this relationship in the aquarium. The anemones that serve as clownfish hosts in nature are notoriously difficult to keep alive in the aquarium—even for the experts. Fortunately, clownfish will get along just fine in captivity without a host anemone being present.

The only problem you might encounter when keeping a clownfish without an anemone host is that it might misdirect its instinct to take refuge in an anemone by nestling within the tentacles of LPS corals or other long-tentacled invertebrates, which may prove irritating to the proxy host.

Common clowns and many other clownfish species will readily accept a wide range of foods, including live or frozen brine shrimp, chopped bits of seafood, flakes, and frozen or freeze-dried zooplankton.

The Damsels

Close cousins to the clownfish, the damsels are also ideal mini-reef inhabitants in that they will not usually nibble at or otherwise molest sessile invertebrates. Being among the hardiest reef fish available, they are extremely easy for even novice reef keepers to maintain. In addition, damsels will thrive on all the same easy-to-provide fare described above for clownfish.

Small schooling fishes like this Green Chromis make excellent mini-reef residents.

The damsels' one drawback is their aforementioned penchant for pugnacity, which can make life unbearable for smaller or more passive tankmates. However, one particular species, the Yellowtail Blue Damsel (*Chrysiptera parasema*) tends to be far less aggressive than many of its relatives, provided it is introduced last or at the same time as the other fish. When introduced in this fashion, the only aggressiveness I've observed from this species toward tankmates is some mild displaying and occasional half-hearted chasing.

C. parasema is a dazzling little jewel to behold, especially under metal halide lighting, which really seems to make its cobalt blue and yellow coloration "pop" and to bring out the iridescent red highlights that edge its scales and crisscross its face.

The Royal Gramma

The Royal Gramma (*Gramma loreto*) was, I believe, specifically designed to serve as the perfect mini-reef inhabitant. *G. loreto* will coexist peacefully with most other reef-friendly species, showing aggression only toward conspecifics and interlopers attempting to invade its cave in the rockwork, which it will defend with vigor. Though, as a rule, *G. loreto* should be stocked only one to a tank, some aquarists have succeeded in maintaining groups of these fish in very large systems.

The Royal Gramma is a colorful and very popular species that is suitable for most mini-reef setups.

G. loreto seldom strays far from its chosen cave, which it will often inhabit, curiously enough, while oriented upside down. A planktonivore by nature, this beautiful fish feeds by dashing out of hiding and engulfing zooplankton drifting by in the current. In the aquarium, it should be offered a variety of live and frozen meaty foods, but it will also heartily accept flakes and freeze-dried offerings as well.

The Royal Gramma's coloration is quite cheerful, looking as if the front half of the fish were dipped in purple Easter egg dye and the back half in yellow. This remarkable coloration tends to fade when water conditions begin to deteriorate, making *G. loreto* something of an aquatic canary in the coal mine. However, please do not wait until your Royal Gramma's intense colors begin to fade before performing a routine water change!

A close relative of the Royal Gramma that is equally desirable in the mini-reef (if not quite as commonly available) is the Blackcap Basslet (*Gramma melacara*). A denizen of deeper reefs, the Blackcap Basslet has a similarly peaceful disposition and can be trained to accept the same food items as *G. loreto.*

The Firefish

Two species of firefish, *Nemateleotris decora* and *N. magnifica*, are also great choices for the mini-reef, provided they are housed with non-aggressive tankmates. Abundant hiding places should be provided so that these shy fish always have "bolt holes" to retreat to when they feel threatened.

N. decora has an elongated body that is predominately yellow with vibrant-purple fins. *N. magnifica* has a similar body plan but exhibits yellowish-red coloration across its posterior half. Also, *N. magnifica's* initial dorsal ray is significantly more elongated and curved than that of *N. decora*.

Like *Gramma loreto*, the firefish are planktonivores, which hover above the rockwork and wait for zooplankton to drift by. In the mini-reef, they should be offered a variety of live and frozen meaty foods, such as vitamin-enriched brine shrimp, mysis shrimp, and finely chopped seafood. Keep an eye out for faster tankmates that continually out-compete your firefish at feeding time, or else they might starve.

I should point out that firefish are incredible jumpers and are able to leap through the smallest opening in an aquarium's cover. Too often, such acrobatics go unnoticed by the aquarist until it's too late and the firefish winds up facing a dusty demise on the fish room floor. As you've probably surmised, a tight-fitting cover glass is necessary if you plan to keep firefish.

The Mandarinfish and Psychedelic Fish

Many experienced reef keepers out there would likely want to pillory me for including the Mandarinfish

The Purple Firefish is a great choice for hobbyists looking for something a little different.

The Common Firefish is easily identified by the orangey-red posterior of its body.

The Mandarin is popular with mini-reefers of all experience levels.

Psychedelic Mandarins need plenty of small live invertebrates to thrive in your mini reef.

(*Synchiropus splendidus*) and the closely related Psychedelic Mandarinfish (*Synchiropus picturatus*) in a list of beginner-friendly reef fish. These fish have an abysmal survival rate in newly set up tanks and in tanks that lack sufficient quantities of high-quality live rock and/or live sand.

You see, *S. splendidus* and *S. picturatus* feed exclusively on the tiny amphipods, copepods, and other microfauna found on or within live rock and live sand. While some who have kept these fish have succeeded in weaning them onto live brine shrimp and other live foods, many more have watched helplessly as the fish slowly wasted away after having consumed all the available microfauna in the system.

Okay, so why am I listing these fish if they are so hard to keep alive? Well, the truth of the matter is, they're not that difficult to maintain. You just have to make sure that their food supply never runs out! That means providing a large aquarium (75-100 gallons or more) with ample live rock and allowing it to mature for no less than six months before adding one of these fish. As additional insurance that the food supply will hold out, a refugium could be added to the mini-reef system.

If you conscientiously satisfy these requirements and don't cut any corners, a Mandarinfish or Psychedelic fish will reward you with its peculiar beauty for years. And what beauties they are! Verbal descriptions seldom do justice to these wildly patterned and extravagantly colored fish, but the word "psychedelic" is certainly apropos.

The bodies of *S. splendidus* and *S. picturatus* are coated with toxic mucus, so other fish tend to leave them alone. They,

Part 4

too, will completely ignore their tankmates as they flit about from rock to rock, looking very much like underwater versions of the hummingbird. However, males of both species will not suffer the presence of conspecific males lightly, so they should be stocked only one to a tank.

The Yellow Tang

The Yellow Tang (*Zebrasoma flavescens*) is a welcome addition to the larger mini-reef (75 gallons or more) with ample swimming area. Its unrivaled brilliant-yellow coloration makes a dramatic visual statement, and it will coexist peacefully with most other reef fish, with the exception of conspecifics and other tang species.

Take care when handling this species, however. Like all tangs and surgeonfish, it possesses scalpel-like spines on the caudal peduncle (the area just in front of its tail) that are capable of inflicting a painful wound.

Being herbivorous, *Z. flavescens* is often introduced to the mini-reef as a means of controlling filamentous algae. However, its track record in this area is mixed at best. My specimen will occasionally nibble at hair algae, but it seems to find it less than palatable and does very little to slow its growth.

Yellow Tangs must be allowed to graze continuously on algae throughout the day, and they will suffer in captivity if they lack an outlet for this natural behavior–or they will misdirect it by nipping at the tissues of some LPS corals and the mantles of *Tridacna* clams. A steady supply of dried nori (the seaweed used to wrap sushi) is ideal for this purpose. You can get a package of nori for just a few dollars at any Oriental food market. Dried red marine algae, which also comes in sheets, is accepted with gusto as well. Just tear off a section of nori or red algae, clamp it in a lettuce feeder or algae magnet, place it in your mini-reef, and your tang will graze on it all day long.

Yellow Tangs do well in larger mini-reef setups. Be sure to feed them plenty of greens!

cardinalfishes make interesting mini-reef inhabitants. The Banggai Cardinalfish is pictured here.

For those hobbyists with a deep substrate, jawfishes are unique and interesting to observe.

And the List Goes On...

As I mentioned, this is only a partial list of fish that are suitable for inclusion in the mini-reef. You might also want to experiment with one or more of the following species:

• Midas Blenny (*Ecsenius midas*)

• Banggai Cardinalfish (*Pterapogon kauderni*)

• Pajama Cardinalfish (*Sphaeramia nematoptera*)

• Longnose Hawkfish (*Oxycirrhites typus*)

• Pixy Hawkfish (*Cirrhitichthys oxycephalus*)

• Dusky Jawfish (*Opistognathus whitehurstii*)

• Yellowhead Jawfish (*Opistognathus aurifrons*)

20

Motile Invertebrates in the Mini-Reef

Up until now, we've focused our discussion of marine invertebrates primarily on sessile species. But many motile invertebrates–those that are capable of moving around the aquarium freely–make excellent additions to the mini-reef as well. Some motile invertebrates are worth incorporating for their aesthetic qualities, while others serve a more practical function in the mini-reef. Still others combine the qualities of beauty and practicality.

Little Shrimps with Prawn-Sized Personalities

The first group of motile invertebrates that springs to mind is the cleaner shrimps, four of which routinely appear in dealers' display tanks. The

Perhaps a little too motile, Flame Scallops can bounce all over the mini-reef, knocking corals over.

Blood Shrimp make very colorful additions to the mini-reef aquarium.

cleaner shrimps are so named because in nature, they "staff" coral reef cleaning stations where fish—even big, predatory species—line up to be picked clean of parasites and dead tissue. These shrimps are great fun to interact with in the mini-reef because they will actually direct their cleaning attention to the aquarist's hand if it is placed nearby.

Obviously, the mini-reef offers far fewer opportunities for cleaner shrimps to pick parasites, but fortunately, they will quickly learn to accept a variety of frozen and dry foods, including brine shrimp, finely chopped seafood, flakes, freeze-dried plankton, and just about anything else you might introduce. In fact, the bits of food left over by your fish will often suffice for these non-finicky feeders.

Blood Shrimp

I'll start with my personal favorite: the blood shrimp (*Lysmata debelius*). This gorgeous shrimp has a blood-red body accented with white polka dots on its carapace. Its antennae and legs are also white—the latter giving the amusing impression that the shrimp is wearing knee-high white stockings.

Incidentally, the long, flowing antennae possessed by the Blood Shrimp and other cleaner shrimps serve an important purpose apart from helping these shrimps sense their surroundings. That is, they "advertise" to potential "clients" that these animals are in the cleaning business.

When introduced to the mini-reef, this deep-water species may be shy at first, retiring to a cave in the rockwork during daylight hours. However, its confidence will soon build, and it will spend more time out in the open. These stunning shrimps can safely be kept in small groups.

White-banded Cleaner Shrimp

A close second to the Blood Shrimp when it comes to looks is the White-banded Cleaner Shrimp (*Lysmata amboinensis*). Predominately yellow in coloration, *L. amboinensis* sports a bold swath of red down its back with a brilliant white stripe running through the middle.

Like *L. debelius, L. amboinensis* does quite well in small groups.

Peppermint Shrimp

We've already discussed the Peppermint Shrimp (*Lysmata wurdemanni*) in terms of its *Aiptasia*-eating proclivity, which is a tremendous bonus for reef keepers. But this shrimp is more than just a member of the crustacean cleanup crew. In fact, it's quite beautiful and fascinating in its own right–whether it chooses to gobble up *Aiptasia* or not!

As its common name suggests, the Peppermint Shrimp's coloration and patterning are similar to peppermint candy, which is quite whimsical in a living thing.

L. wurdemanni does best when stocked in small groups and prefers the company of peaceful tank mates over rambunctious reef residents. In fact, this species may go into hiding if it shares a tank with a lively community of fish.

Banded Coral Shrimp

Looking rather like a tiny barber's pole with ten legs and ridiculously long antennae, the Banded Coral Shrimp (*Stenopus hispidus*) has become something of a mini-reef mainstay. This shrimp is completely inoffensive to sessile invertebrates and seldom quarrelsome with motile tankmates even though it is quite well endowed in the claw area. However, *S hispidus* can be quite scrappy with conspecifics and so should be stocked one to a tank. The only exception to this rule is when keeping mated pairs, which are occasionally collected and sold together. Like *L. debelius,* the Banded

Cleaner shrimps, such as this Skunk Cleaner, do well in small groups.

The Peppermint Shrimp is often available at a fraction of the price of the other cleaner shrimps.

Part 4

This Bat Star is a brightly-colored starfish species that is generally harmless in mini-reefs.

Coral Shrimp may be shy and retiring at first but will soon emerge from hiding with regularity.

Superstars of the Mini-Reef

Many outstanding candidates for the mini-reef can be found among the phylum Echinodermata, including many of the brittlestars and serpent stars, several sea stars (a.k.a., starfish), and even a few of the sea urchins.

On the other hand, I would strongly caution the novice reefer against including certain echinoderms in the mini-reef–even if they are offered for sale–due to their highly specialized feeding habits or their "toxic personalities."

Among the former, you have the feather stars (or crinoids), which are filter feeders that demand a continuous supply of tiny live plankton–a condition that is virtually impossible for the average aquarist to replicate.

Among the latter, you have many of the sea cucumbers. While some sea cucumbers are perfectly suited for life in the mini-reef, all of these animals are capable of exuding a toxin called holothurin, which can wipe out everything in the system. Sea cucumbers also have the capacity to discharge their viscera when stressed, producing a sticky, threadlike substance that can foul the aquarium and entangle its inhabitants.

The sea apples exhibit the best (or should I say worst) of both worlds in that they are specialized filter feeders that are capable of releasing toxins and everting their innards. Sea apples, as exquisitely beautiful as they are, are best left to the experts, or better yet, left in the ocean. All that being said, let's take a look at the true superstars of the mini-reef.

Brittle Stars and Serpent Stars

The brittle stars and serpent stars make superb additions to the mini-reef. These close relatives of the sea stars possess five very slender, flexible arms, which radiate from a relatively small central disk. Species with spines along their arms, such as *Ophiarachna incrassata* (the Green Brittle Star), are categorized as brittle stars, while those with smooth arms, such as *Ophioderma squamosissimus* (the Red Serpent Star) are commonly called serpent stars.

Unlike their sea star cousins, which move along almost imperceptibly, the brittle stars are capable of fairly rapid movement–sometimes even scrambling out from hiding to secure food items before competition arrives. Those aquarists with arachnophobic tendencies (fear of spiders) may find the spider-like appearance and movement of these echinoderms somewhat disconcerting.

Red Serpent Stars are probably the most popular of the ornamental starfishes.

Most brittle stars and serpent stars feed on detritus, uneaten food, and even feces, and they are in no way harmful to sessile invertebrates–hence their suitability for the mini-reef environment. However, the aforementioned *O. incrassata* is capable of capturing and devouring small fish.

At first glance, you might think the brittle stars are inappropriately named, as their bodies appear quite sturdy. But when handled by the aquarist or harassed by predators, their arms tend to break off quite easily. Broken arms will, however, regenerate rapidly.

Sea Stars
A few excellent candidates for the mini-reef can be found among the sea stars–the more robust-bodied cousins of the brittle stars and serpent stars–but species must be selected with considerable care, as many will gleefully gorge themselves on coral polyps and the tissues of other sessile invertebrates.

Also, as a rule, sea stars must be very gradually acclimated to the mini-reef if they are to survive the transition, and their specific dietary needs must be very thoroughly researched and diligently provided.

Though it's an imprecise guideline, you can safely rule out most of the sea star species that

Brittle Stars make great additions to the mini-reef aquarium.

There are many types of sea urchins, some more suitable than others.

have knobbed "backs," such as the Chocolate Chip Sea Star (*Protoreaster nodosus*) and the Red-Knobbed Sea Star (*Protoreaster lincki*), as they generally cannot be trusted around sessile invertebrates. However, smooth-skinned species generally will not harm sessile invertebrates.

Some good choices for the mini-reef include the Blue Sea Star (*Linckia laevigata*), the Red Sea Star (*Fromia elegans*), and the Comet Sea Star (*Linckia multifora*). Each grazes primarily on detritus and algae and will accept occasional offerings of finely chopped seafood.

Sea Urchins
Usually introduced to the mini-reef as a means of controlling algae, these spiny echinoderms also have a certain subtle beauty that many reefers find appealing. As with the sea stars, not all sea urchins are equally suitable for the mini-reef, but some species are welcome additions and more than earn their keep by devouring nuisance algae.

One admonition, though: While most sea urchins are primarily herbivorous, some species will occasionally shift their diets to include coral polyps–just as the low-carb dieter will occasionally binge on potato chips. So, urchins in the mini-reef must be observed carefully to ensure that they don't get caught with their spines in the coral polyp cookie jar.

Some of the better choices of urchin for the mini-reef include the Rock-Boring Urchin (and yes, it does bore holes in live rock) (*Echinometra mathaei*), the Globe Urchin (*Mespilia globulus*), and the Jewel Urchin (*Salmacis bicolor*).

The long-spined urchins of the genus *Diadema* are best left out of the mini-reef. Not only do they sometimes feed on sessile invertebrates, but they can also inflict painful stings with their exceptionally long, venomous spines. In addition, the long-spined varieties can really nettle their invertebrate neighbors in the close confines of the mini-reef. While wielding shorter spines and being generally safe around sessile invertebrates, the Sea Egg Urchin (*Tripneustes ventricosus*) is another venomous species capable of dishing out an excruciating sting.

Careful With Crabs!

Most of the so-called true crabs get too large and rambunctious for inclusion in the mini-reef. So, when shopping for motile invertebrates for your system, be wary of purchasing any "mystery" crab specimens. The same applies to collecting your own specimens–perhaps from a tidal pool during a trip to the seashore. That small, cute specimen of uncertain taxonomy might turn into your worst nightmare once it reaches full size and begins to wreak havoc in your mini-reef!

Dwarf Hermit Crabs

Some diminutive crab species make ideal–even beneficial–mini-reef inhabitants. Take the various dwarf hermit crabs, for instance. Several species within this group of small crabs are commonly introduced to the mini-reef to aid in controlling problem algae. The Mexican Red-Legged Hermit Crab (*Clibanarius digueti*) and the Tricolor Hermit Crab (*Clibanarius tricolor*) are very frequently introduced for this purpose. The Scarlet Hermit Crab (*Paguristes cadenati*) is another good algae eater that is quite attractive with its bright red body and yellow eye stalks. Each of these hermits is just slightly larger than one inch at maturity.

The Red-legged Hermit Crab is a must-have for the mini-reef.

The only drawback to using the dwarf hermits for algae control is that they must be stocked in large numbers if they are to be effective–some experts recommend stocking as many as one crab per gallon of aquarium capacity (or even more!). That's an awful lot of little crabs stumbling around your mini-reef–and over your corals and other sessile invertebrates.

Emerald Crabs are excellent choices for controlling bubble algae.

And keep in mind that not all hermit crabs are dwarfs or reef safe. Like the "true crabs," many hermits can get quite large and predatory. For example, the Red Hermit Crab (*Dardanus megistos*) reaches a whopping 12 inches at maturity–a pity for us reef keepers, since *D. megistos* happens to be a great *Aiptasia* eater!

Emerald Crab

Another crab that has been known to serve a useful function in the mini-reef is the Emerald Crab, or Emerald *Mithrax* Crab (*Mithrax sculptus*). So named for its shiny green body, the Emerald Crab is often touted for its tendency to devour bubble algae (*Velonia* spp.), a troublesome form of algae that can rapidly spread throughout the aquarium. Some aquarists report great success in controlling bubble algae with this crab, while others have no luck at all getting their *M. sculptus* to consume the stuff. I've also read that this species can become problematic as it gets larger, consuming coral polyps and even small fish. Hence, the Emerald Crab should be monitored carefully for such "misbehavior."

Sally Lightfoot Crab

Besides sharing its last name with a legendary folk singer, the delightful little Sally Lightfoot Crab (*Percnon gibbesi*) is one of the few truly crab-like crabs that are welcome in the mini-reef.

Reaching just a little over two inches in mature size, the Sally Lightfoot Crab is primarily herbivorous–though it may opportunistically catch and eat small fish.

While not the most colorful crab on the block, *P. gibbesi* is a little bundle of energy that is hilarious to observe–especially for kids. Its flattened body continually skitters about the rockwork, and its claws are in perpetual motion, plucking at the tiny bits of algae growing in the cracks and crevices. This crab also sports tiny appendages above each eye that continually flick up and down. I might also add that its molted exoskeletons–which remain almost perfectly intact–make excellent fodder for practical jokes, but that's all I'll say on that subject.

Part 4

Porcelain Crabs and Coral Crabs

Several miniature crab species make their homes among the stinging tentacles of anemones or among the branches of stony corals and therefore are ideally suited for the mini-reef that houses their appropriate host invertebrates. These commensal crabs include the porcelain crabs and the coral crabs.

The exoskeletons of the aptly named porcelain crabs have the appearance of shiny porcelain painted with red or brown spots or stripes. These anemone-occupying crabs are primarily filter feeders that use special feathery projections on their mouthparts to sieve particles from the water, but some will accept finely chopped bits of seafood as well. Among the more commonly recognized species are *Neopetrolisthes ohshimai* and *Neopetrolisthes maculatus*.

The coral crabs, such as *Trapezia ferruginea* and *Trapezia wardi*, are also quite attractive–albeit secretive–little crabs. The exoskeleton of *T. wardi* is white with red polka dots, while that of *T. ferruginea* is muted orange. These tiny crabs–about one inch in diameter–feed on the mucus (and particles trapped in the mucus) found on the branches of their stony coral hosts. Rest assured, however, that this feeding behavior is in no way harmful to the corals.

More Agents of Algae Control

As with the dwarf hermit crabs, several snail species are routinely introduced to the mini-reef as agents of algae control rather than for their intrinsic beauty. In fact, many online purveyors of reef livestock sell algae "cleanup crew" packages that include a varied mix of reef-safe, herbivorous snails and hermits.

Such combo packages can be quite useful in eliminating irksome algae, but they also have their drawbacks. The first issue that comes to mind is that these algae cleanup crews usually include a rather large number of specimens–both hermits and snails. Sounds like you're getting your money's worth, right? The problem is, once this army of algae

Turbo Snails can be purchased alone or as part of an "algae cleanup crew."

Part 4

eaters goes to work on you mini-reef, it may rapidly deplete the algae in the system, which means you'll have to reduce the population over time (by trading them with other aquarists) to keep it proportionate with the food supply. Otherwise, the population will limit itself as specimens begin starving to death!

Another drawback to algae cleanup crews is that most of the snails included in these packages are fairly short-lived species anyway. And when snails begin dying off in large numbers, the resultant decomposition of dead specimens that, perhaps, remain unobserved in the rockwork can have a significant impact on water quality.

Their short-lived nature aside, herbivorous snails are a welcome addition to the mini-reef, as the right mix of species will help to control the growth of diatoms, film algae, filamentous algae, and cyanobacteria. The "right mix" might include species of nerite snails (such as *Nerita funiculata* and *N. albicilla*), cerith snails (such as *Cerithium strercusmuscarum*), turban snails (such as *Turbo brunneus*), and *Astraea* snails (such as *Astraea tecta*).

Don't Pull Your Hair Out Over Algae!

Contending with troublesome algae is a fact of life for reef keepers. We reefers must continually maintain a delicate balance between nutrient import and export, proper stocking and overstocking, proper feeding and overfeeding, as well as proper illumination and overillumination, lest our thriving mini-reefs become overrun with problem algae growth.

But just what is "problem algae"? After all, myriad forms of algae are found on natural coral reefs. Why attempt to check their growth in the mini-reef? To find the answer to that question, let's revisit the gardening analogy I introduced in the first chapter of this book.

Controlling problem algae is just one task involved in the success of your mini-reef.

Caulerpa is often used in refugiums as a nutrient sponge.

Aquatic "Weeds"

A garden or flowerbed is typically planted with a variety of ornamental species selected for the attractiveness of their blooms or foliage–and often from disparate ecological niches. Few gardeners strive to recreate a truly natural combination of plants. "Ornamental" species simply cannot dominate the garden setting that is shared by more invasive and aggressive "weed" species.

While not a perfect analogy, one can certainly recognize that the average mini-reef incorporates sessile invertebrates from different zones on the reef– and even from different parts of the world–and that, for most reef keepers, aesthetics tend to figure in more prominently than natural origins when selecting livestock. Hence, allowing ugly, invasive algae species to take hold in the mini-reef is generally considered undesirable. (Incidentally, it's this same principle that makes *Aiptasia* anemones so unappealing to reef aquarists.)

Besides, on the natural reefs, algae growth is usually kept in check via the staggering number and diversity of herbivorous fish and motile invertebrates–a state of affairs that is impossible to duplicate in the closed system of the mini-reef, where the biological load must be kept to a minimum.

So, to answer my earlier question, "problem algae" can be defined as any form of algae that detracts from the aesthetic beauty of the mini-reef and/or out-competes the corals and other sessile invertebrates for space in the system. Algae growths are a "problem" only in the sense that, much like terrestrial weed plants, they occur where we don't want them to occur.

Meet the "Big Four"

The "big four" forms of problem algae that are routinely encountered in the reef keeping hobby include diatoms, cyanobacteria (a.k.a. slime algae or blue-green algae), green filamentous algae (a.k.a. "hair algae"), and bubble algae.

So what are the characteristics of the big four, and how can you go about controlling them? Let's explore each form in the order you're likely to experience it.

A Natural Progression

Before we go any further, I should point out that a newly established reef system will go through a natural progression of algae blooms–from diatoms to cyanobacteria to hair algae–as the system matures. Each bloom will resolve itself naturally within a matter of weeks as nutrients are used up, so don't let this completely natural phase alarm you! However, I would strongly encourage you to hold off stocking any corals or other invertebrates until the cycle is completely finished. Otherwise, the additional bioload and resultant dissolved organic compounds will only prolong the process.

Although this initial progression of algae blooms is normal and expected, recurring algae blooms are an indication that adjustments in husbandry techniques are needed.

Diatoms

Diatoms are the first algae you'll encounter as your newly set up system begins to cycle. This form appears as a golden-brown film on the glass. It's fairly easy to dislodge using an algae magnet or scraper, but tends to reappear a day or so later.

Diatoms require silicates for survival and so may become problematic in systems where non-purified tap water (often found to contain silicates) is used.

Diatoms are relatively easy to control through routine aquarium maintenance, and the introduction of a few herbivorous snails, such as the aforementioned *Astraea* species, will go a long way toward keeping your glass crystal clear.

Cyanobacteria

As the name suggests, the various species of cyanobacteria (a.k.a., blue-green algae or slime algae) are not true algae at all but rather are bacteria. This form usually manifests itself as slimy red, black, or green sheets that appear on the rockwork and substrate. The sheets are loosely attached and therefore occasionally rise to the surface of the aquarium.

Cyanobacteria thrive in areas of minimal water movement when dissolved nutrient levels are high. Control is achieved through increasing water movement in the affected part of the system and increasing nutrient export via aggressive protein skimming and water changes.

Some aquarists recommend using antibiotics, such as erythromycin, to control cyanobacteria, but I would caution against it. After all, what happens to the colonies of beneficial nitrifying and denitrifying bacteria that we depend upon so heavily when an antibiotic is introduced to the system? The potential disruption in biological filtration is just not worth it when a cyanobacteria bloom can so easily be brought under control through modifications in husbandry techniques.

Hair Algae

The third type of algae you'll encounter is also the most irksome–hair algae. I suspect that more reef keepers have abandoned the mini-reef hobby because of repeated outbreaks of hair algae than for any other reason.

Several forms of filamentous green algae are lumped under the broader heading of "hair algae." The various species may be hair-like, feathery, or turf-like in appearance, and all forms are extremely challenging to eradicate.

Hair algae is fueled by intense lighting coupled with dissolved nutrients, such as nitrate and phosphate. Unlike cyanobacteria, it thrives in areas of high water movement. If allowed to proliferate unchecked, hair algae can completely overrun a mini-reef and smother the sessile invertebrates.

The most important aspect of hair algae control involves increasing nutrient export while decreasing nutrient import. The former is achieved with purified tap water, stepped-up water changes, vigorous protein skimming, and other forms of water purification, while the latter is achieved through careful monitoring of food items that are introduced to the system and by stocking the system at appropriate levels.

Introducing macroalgae, such as the various *Halimeda* and *Caulerpa* species, to the mini-reef can also assist with nutrient export. Macroalgae is grown either in the main system or in a refugium and is routinely pruned to keep its growth under control. The macroalgae takes up the nutrients that would otherwise fuel hair algae, and pruning effectively removes the nutrients from the system.

Since hair algae thrives under intense illumination, it's essential to avoid leaving the lights on for excessive amounts of time. Realistically, you can't cut your photoperiod back too much or your photosynthetic invertebrates will begin to suffer. However, you can put your lights on a timer to ensure that they aren't, say, left on several hours longer than necessary when you're away from home longer than expected.

Manually removing clumps of hair algae also helps to reduce its presence in your mini-reef. Brushing the algae from the rocks and from around your invertebrates with a soft-bristled toothbrush is also helpful. However, any algae liberated through brushing must be siphoned promptly from the water, or else you will succeed only in spreading more of the stuff around the aquarium. This can be quite a challenge, as you almost need to brush and siphon simultaneously to keep little bits from drifting throughout the tank.

Finally, your attack on hair algae should also include herbivorous fish and motile invertebrates, such as the Convict Tang (*Acanthurus triostegus*), the Foxface (*Lo vulpinus*), Astraea snails, and Mexican Red-legged Hermit Crabs (*Clibanarius digueti*).

Just be aware that few organisms will eat long growths of filamentous green algae, because the longer it grows, the tougher it gets. That being said, herbivorous fish and invertebrates will help to prevent recurrences of hair algae after you've plucked and brushed away as much of the nasty green stuff as you can. Also, keep in mind that whenever you add organisms–even if it is for the purpose of algae control–you are also adding more dissolved pollutants to the system, which, as we know, can promote further algae growth.

Sound overwhelming? Well, overcoming a hair algae outbreak can be quite frustrating, but you can rest assured that your persistence will pay off. If you stick with these principles, you will ultimately succeed in vanquishing this filamentous foe–and you won't end up pulling your own hair out in the process!

Bubble Algae

While a bubble algae outbreak is not part of the initial series of blooms you will encounter as your system matures, this prolific form of algae commonly arrives in the mini-reef as a live rock stowaway.

This aptly named algae has the appearance of small, green, semi-translucent bubbles,

Part 4

ranging from about the size of a pea to the size of a marble (some even achieve shooter marble dimensions!) One could argue that bubble algae (*Valonia* and *Dictosphaeria* spp.) is rather attractive and interesting looking. In fact, reef aquarists in some parts of the world will actually pay for live rock covered with the stuff. The only trouble is, bubble algae, like hair algae, can overrun the aquarium, even attaching itself to the skeletons of LPS and SPS corals.

Unfortunately, you can't starve bubble algae out of existence or control it by reducing illumination. Your best bet is to pick the bubbles gently by hand as soon as they appear. Gently is the operative word here. If you pluck them too forcefully, you will rupture the delicate membrane, releasing hundreds of spores into the system, and thereby exacerbating the problem.

As I mentioned in the previous chapter, emerald crabs have been known to eat bubble algae–but not reliably. Some fish, including various tang species, have also been observed munching on this form of algae, but again, you can't count on them to develop a taste for it.

The bottom line when it comes to controlling bubble algae: You might just have to get "picky" about it!

22

Enjoying the Fruits of Your Labor

Let me be the first to congratulate you as you embark on a remarkable new hobby! By merely taking the time to read this book, you've already demonstrated that you're willing to learn before you leap, which will pay huge dividends in the form of a thriving mini-reef ecosystem.

However, this book is just a ripple on the surface of all there is to learn and discover about reef keeping—and that's one reason this hobby is so exciting! Such a wealth of information is available in literature and online that you can spend a lifetime researching this topic and never come close to learning all there is to know! My hope is that this book has piqued your interest just

Hard work and dedication will produce a beautiful mini-reef for years to come.

enough to make you want to delve even deeper into the many outstanding marine aquarium references out there.

As you consider the different approaches to reef keeping and weigh the myriad opinions you're likely to come across, always keep in mind that there's no "right" way to reef. There are numerous roads to reef-keeping success, and the techniques that work for one aquarist may not work for another. Don't fall into the trap of changing your husbandry approach with every new reef-keeping fad, because methods that are considered dogma one year may be considered heresy the next!

Now that you've got the mini-reef bug, the only cure is to indulge your aquatic appetite! So, why not dive right in and begin the adventure of a lifetime? There's no question that the mini-reef hobby can be challenging, but I know you're up to it—and I hope you'll enjoy the reef-keeping experience for many years to come.

Resources

Organizations

Federation of American Aquarium Societies (FAAS)

Secretary: Jane Benes

E-mail: Jbenes01@yahoo.com

www.gcca.net/faas

Federation of British Aquatic Societies (FBAS)

Secretary: Vivienne Pearce

E-mail: Webmaster@fbas.co.uk

www.fbas.co.uk

International Marinelife Alliance (IMA)

President: Vaughan R. Pratt

E-mail: info@ma

rine.org

www.marine.org

Marine Aquarium Council (MAC)

923 Nu'uanu Avenue

Honolulu, HI 96817

Telephone: (808) 550-8217

Fax: (808) 550-8317

E-mail: info@aquariumcouncil.org

www.aquariumcouncil.org

Marine Aquarium Societies of North America (MASNA)

Director of Membership/Secretary: Cheri Phillips

E-mail: cheri@uniquesensations.com

www.masna.org

ReefGuardian International

2829 Bird Avenue-Suite 5

PMB 162

Miami, FL 33133-4668

E-mail: info@ReefGuardian.org

www.reefguardian.org

The Coral Reef Alliance

417 Montgomery Street, Suite 205

San Francisco, CA 94104

Telephone: (888) CORAL-REEF

Fax: (415) 834-0999

E-mail: info@coral.org

www.coralreefalliance.org

The International Federation of Online Clubs and Aquatic Societies (IFOCAS)

E-mail: ifocas@ifocas.fsworld.co.uk

www.ifocas.fsworld.co.uk

Publications

Tropical Fish Hobbyist magazine

The Leading Aquarium Magazine For Over Half a Century
www.tfhmagazine.com

Tropical Fish Hobbyist magazine has been the source of accurate, up-to-the-minute, fascinating information on every facet of the aquarium hobby including freshwater fish, aquatic plants, marine aquaria, mini-reefs, and ponds for over 50 years. *TFH* will take you to new heights with its informative articles and stunning photos. With thousands of fish, plants, and other underwater creatures available, the hobbyist needs levelheaded advice about their care, maintenance, and breeding. *TFH* authors have the knowledge and experience to help make your aquarium sensational.

T.F.H. Publications, Inc.
1 TFH Plaza
Third & Union Avenues
Neptune City, NJ 07753
Telephone: 1-888-859-9034
E-mail: info@tfh.com

Internet Resources

AquaLink

(www.aqualink.com)

The largest aquaria web resource in the world, AquaLink provides fishkeepers with information on a variety of topics, including freshwater and marine fish, aquatic plants, goldfish, reef systems, invertebrates, and corals.

Aquaria Central

(www.aquariacentral.com)

Aquaria Central is an online resource offering species profiles, help forums, chat rooms, and a variety of aquaria articles. To date, there are more than 700 species profiles listed on this website's searchable database.

AquariumHobbyist

(www.aquariumhobbyist.com)

This website lists upcoming marine-related events, as well as commercial pages, chat rooms, news, a classifieds section, and care information.

Reef Central

(www.reefcentral.com)

Reef Central is an online community that shares information regarding the marine and reef aquarium hobby. The site includes access to discussion forums, photo galleries, chat rooms, and news.

Reefs.Org

(www.reefs.org)

An online interactive community, Reefs.Org is home to an active bulletin board, reference library, chat room, monthly periodical, and online curriculum.

Wet Web Media

(www.wetwebmedia.com)

This website features extensive aquarium, fish, and aquatic information, with numerous articles on marine aquariums, freshwater aquariums, aquarium plants, ponds, and other related topics.

Bibliography

Borneman, Eric H.
Aquarium Corals: Selection, Husbandry, and Natural History.
T.F.H./Microcosm Professional Series,
Neptune City, NJ, 2001.

Calfo, Anthony R.
Book of Coral Propagation, Volume 1: Reef Gardening for Aquarists.
Reading Trees Publications,
PO Box 446 Monroeville, PA, 2001.

Michael, Scott W.
Marine Fishes: 500+ Essential-to-Know Aquarium Species.
T.F.H./Microcosm Professional Series,
Neptune City, NJ, 2001.

Michael, Scott W.
Reef Fishes, Volume 1.
T.F.H./Microcosm Professional Series,
Neptune City, NJ, 2001.

Nilsen, Alf Jacob and Fossa, Svein A.
Reef Secrets.
T.F.H./Microcosm Professional Series,
Neptune City, NJ, 2002.

Tullock, John H.
Natural Reef Aquariums: Simplified Approaches to Creating Living Saltwater Microcosms.
T.F.H./Microcosm Professional Series,
Neptune City, NJ, 2001.

Tullock, John H.
The Reef Aquarium Owner's Manual.
Aardvark Press,
PO Box 37571, Valyland 7979,
Cape Town, South Africa, 1993.

Photo Credits

Aaron Norman, 175, 177

Bob Goemans, 21, 30, 60, 144

Coral Reef Ecosystems, 13, 86-87

Courtney Platt, 183

David Herlong, 82, 84, 92-93 (T),

Dr. Z. Takacs, 103

Dupla Aquaristik, 95, 108, 110

G.W. Lange, 79

James Fatherree, 23-24, 31-32, 35, 39-40, 42, 48, 77, 82-83, 85, 99, 116, 118, 120, 125, 127-129, 131-132, 135, 139, 140, 143, 147-157, 161-162, 164-165, 167-168, 174, 185 (B), 188-190, 193-194

John O'Malley, 45, 47, 56, 65, 93, 187

K. Choo, 53

Mark Smith, 54-55, 61, 173, 179 (T), 180 (B), 182 (L), 184, 185 (T), 186, 191

Mary Sweeney, 29

Michael S. Paletta, 28, 44, 49, 106

M.P. & C. Piednoir, 16, 25, 51-52, 81, 91, 115, 174, 182 (R),

Oliver Lucanus, 160

Phillip Hunt, 94, 178

Richard T. Bell, 36, 59

T.F.H. Archives, 14, 27, 41, 64, 69, 72, 97-98, 111, 169, 179 (B), 180 (T), 181

U.E. Friese, 15, 63, 68, 70, 100, 105

Walt Deas, 109

Index